Njongonkulu Ndungane is the Archbishop of Cape Town and the son and grandson of Anglican clergy in South Africa. He began adult life as a political activist and was imprisoned for three years on Robben Island, where he discovered his calling to the priesthood and his conviction that the enemy to confront was poverty. A patron of the Jubilee 2000 movement, the Archbishop has consistently campaigned for the cancellation of unpayable debts owed by developing countries. He is deeply committed to the fight against the abuse of women and children, and plays a leading role in the campaign to eradicate HIV and AIDS in Africa. Archbishop Ndungane is in demand as a speaker and broadcaster in the United Kingdom and throughout the world.

A World with a Human Face

A Voice from Africa

NJONGONKULU NDUNGANE

First published in Africa in 2003 by
David Philip, an imprint of New Africa Books (Pty) Ltd
99 Garfield Road
Kenilworth, Cape Town
South Africa

Every effort has been made to acknowledge fully the sources of material
reproduced in this book. The publisher apologizes for any omissions that
may remain and, if notified, will ensure that full acknowledgements are made
in a subsequent edition.

Scripture quotations are from the New Revised Standard Version of the Bible,
copyright © 1946, 1952 and 1971 by the Division of Christian Education
of the National Council of the Churches of Christ in the USA, and used
by permission; and from the New Jerusalem Bible, published and copyright
© 1985 by Darton, Longman & Todd Ltd and Doubleday, a division of
Random House Inc. and used by permission.

British Library Cataloguing-in-Publication Data
A catalogue record for this book is available from the British Library

ISBN 0–86486–614–3

10 9 8 7 6 5 4 3 2 1

Typeset by Wilmaset Ltd, Birkenhead, Wirral
Printed in Great Britain by MPG Books Ltd, Bodmin, Cornwall

To those who have so little
and deserve so much more

Contents

Acknowledgements

I would like to thank Margaret Legum for reading this book and giving valuable help and feedback as founder of the South African Consultancy CARAS Trust; also Andrew Davey and Peter Sedgwick of the Board for Social Responsibility in London.

Thanks also to Christopher Gregorowski who has made known the African story by James Aggrey, *Fly, Eagle, Fly*.

Much of this book is based on talks and sermons which I have given in many different places: I thank my hosts for invitations that challenged me to formalize and formulate my thoughts on issues close to my heart, and acknowledge their contribution. They include:

- Copenhagen, Denmark: Danish Parliament
- Diakonia Council of Churches
- Durban, South Africa: Biko's Voice for Peace
- Edinburgh, Scotland: Scottish Parliamentarians
- Bremen, Germany
- Glasgow, Scotland
- Los Angeles: Council for World Affairs, USA
- Toronto, Canada: local communities, Global Realities Conference
- Milan, Italy: Jacques Maritain Institute
- Montreal, Canada: Halifax Initiative Coalition
- Morehouse College, USA
- Accra, Ghana: Jubilee 2000, launch of Africa campaign
- CPSA Provincial Synod
- Southwark Cathedral, London
- Berkeley, California: Healing Leaves Conference
- Philadelphia, USA: the 25th anniversary celebration of the ordination of women in the ECUSA
- Worcester State College, USA: honors convocation

There are others too numerous to mention here, whose enthusiastic advice and responses were invaluable. I pray that they know how much their help is appreciated and that I am ever conscious that this book is in many ways the sum of all the parts.

ONE

From Robben Island to Bishopscourt

Every nation's history is shaped by events and by its people. For South Africa, 1960 was a watershed year which unleashed a spiral of events that led 30 years later to the release of Nelson Mandela and the unbanning of political parties. It was a year in which 69 people were killed by the police in Sharpeville for participating in anti-Pass Law demonstrations. It was also the year in which Harold Macmillan, the British Prime Minister at the time, delivered the historic 'Wind of Change' address in the South African parliament. This was a reference to the momentous events that were taking place which would eventually lead to the independence of the continent of Africa. In its editorial on 4 January 1960, the *Rand Daily Mail* wrote:

> The sixties opens in an atmosphere of expectations, a heightened awareness of pending change. In a few years' time Africans will be governing the greater part of the African continent. This will be a decade of great change for the world and for Africa. Can we in South Africa hope to escape the implications?

For me, too, the 1960s brought about a change of course for my life. They marked the beginning of a journey from Robben Island to Bishopscourt, from prisoner to archbishop – a journey that began in chains and has now ended in freedom. This journey began on one Sunday afternoon in Langa, Cape Town. I was on my way to a soccer game when my friends and I stopped to listen to a politician who was addressing an attentive crowd. The politician happened to be Robert Mangaliso Sobukwe, leader of the recently formed Pan Africanist Congress of Azania (PAC). He was in Bhunga Square, Langa, to launch a campaign for the abolition of the Pass Laws which were one of the fundamental pillars of apartheid. These laws were at the very heart of the oppression of black people in South Africa. They determined where black people lived, worked, went to school; whom they might marry and even where they could be buried. In fact, the Pass Laws affected and pass-restricted every facet of life of a black person.

1

These laws were applied with such viciousness and ruthlessness by the apartheid police that the result was a reign of terror in almost all the townships where black people resided.

Sobukwe spoke to these issues with such clarity of mind, passion and purpose that he left no one in doubt about the justness of his cause. Questioned by journalists on his motivation, Sobukwe spoke about the instant arrests to which black men were subjected through the Pass Laws – and with the extension of this system to our womenfolk, it might happen to my mother, my wife, my daughter. 'It is a situation we cannot tolerate any longer. The white man behaves as though he were an occupying power. In order to entrench their privileges, the whites have surrounded themselves with oppressive laws. We have no obligation to obey these laws.'

Sobukwe's eloquence, charisma, decisiveness and clear objectives caught my imagination. Like any person whose conscience has been aroused, I felt I had to stand up and be counted for what I believed was right. That began my long walk in the quest for justice and struggle for liberation. Following the encounter with Robert Sobukwe on 21 March 1960, I became a political activist. This entailed a wide range of activities such as conscientizing people, organizing meetings, educating people about the evils of apartheid, and teaching democratic principles. The political activism that ensued led to my arrest with other PAC adherents and subsequent conviction in August 1963, with a three-year sentence which I served on Robben Island.

Many people were surprised at my getting into trouble. I was a quiet kind of guy who tried to do what was right and to avoid being arrested. They thought it was a big mistake. Of course I had done nothing worthy of arrest and conviction. I was standing up for justice so that everyone can have what is basic for human living in the land of their birth. I was charged for furthering the aims of a banned organization, the Pan Africanist Congress of Azania.

There is a strange paradox about my Robben Island experience. Although we were made to suffer, nevertheless it was a great privilege and honour to be in the company of such outstanding people. No one can take that experience away.

On Robben Island we were together with some great people who were later to play a significant role in shaping the future of South Africa. Chief among them was Nelson Mandela. I always say that my claim to fame is that I built the jail for Mandela. I was there before him and I was involved in the unit that put up the buildings on Robben Island. There was also Stanley Mogoba who later became the Presiding Bishop of the Methodist Church of Southern Africa who on his retirement became President of the PAC. There was Fikile Bam who is now a judge; also Dikgang Moseneke, aged

15 or 16, who was the youngest inmate on Robben Island, and who later qua-
lified as an advocate of the supreme court of South Africa. He is now a judge
in the Constitutional Court. There was Dennis Brutus, an outstanding academic, a poet and activist, a professor at Pittsburgh University and also a
leading figure in the Jubilee 2000 movement and human rights campaign;
also Stix Morewa, one-time top sports administrator in South Africa; Owen
Damoyi, a businessman in Johannesburg; and Wiseman Nkuhlu, Chief Economic Adviser to the President of South Africa.

Relationships across political parties on Robben Island were excellent. We
faced a common enemy and we had to survive together. There was maturity
in our discussions and debates. I recall holding mock rallies in our cells as if we
were preparing for a general election, some even representing the Nationalist
Party, the then governing party in apartheid South Africa. If only we can re-
capture that spirit of togetherness and co-operation as we face a common
challenge in nation building and the eradication of poverty and inequalities!

Today, Robben Island stands as a beacon of hope. Former prisoners under
very inhospitable conditions emerged renewed in their belief in freedom and
justice, committed to a life of service and convinced that lasting peace can
only come through reconciliation and forgiveness.

As a mark of the church's commitment to reconciliation, the Anglican
Church in South Africa has re-consecrated the Church of the Good Shepherd
on Robben Island as a memorial to the transformation process that began
among those forced to quarry stone in the island and now are free – a transformation process that has produced one of the most constitutionally
enlightened democracies in the world. This is a church that was originally
built by Archbishop West Jones about 1878 as a sign of hope for the community of lepers who lived there at the time as a reminder that no people may be
marginalized in the sight of God or their neighbours. We have offered the
Church of the Good Shepherd, a place of ancient ruins with possibilities of
new beginnings, as a symbol of present opportunity and future hope. In our
renovation of that church we have made a statement that we have claimed it as
a place of pilgrimage and reconciliation. The island of incarceration has
become the island of faith.

The potent symbolism of this island of suffering and bitterness is that out
of that you could have someone who could lead South Africa into transformation. It had a positive influence in the world beyond South Africa. It is part of
that spirit of hope, that reconciling effect, that people who were incarcerated
on the island can bring to the world.

It would be the easiest thing in the world to romanticize the notion of the
freedom of the island: to see its new status only as a symbol of a new, good

future. Yes, for that we must strive. But experience teaches us, especially on this island, that it has been used for different purposes of incarceration by different governments, and that history all too often repeats itself.

The journey to the island for the first political prisoners of the Nationalist government was itself an introduction to the callousness of the prison life that awaited us across the bay. We went to Robben Island in chains, handcuffed and chained at the legs. At the harbour, as the manacled prisoners tried to negotiate the tricky gap between the high quay and the heaving deck of the ferry, the guards would prod and shove us. As we were manhandled on to the ferry, it was the darkest of days. It was a terrifying trek across the water.

People tend to romanticize Robben Island, but it was hell on earth. And I have often said that as a young black person, who in the apartheid mindset saw white people as next to angels, seeing the other side of humanity was something of an eye-opener. Yet even among the hard-hearted apartheid warders, there were those who, in a way, got to know who we were. And I recall one who was the head of the building group, who was beginning to say: 'We have tried to break the backs of these people but their spirits are good . . . maybe God is saying something to us?' Of course, when that kind of metamorphosis happened, such a person got transferred. Yet, even within the system, you found people who discovered that humanity.

To me that was a lesson, that there is something in the human spirit, which recognizes our true humanity. People tend to be victims of ideologies and it is the system which imprisons them. Therefore one cannot strike off and condemn people entirely because of the prejudices and backgrounds from which they come. As people get to know each other, transformation takes place and a common humanity is discovered. Among the prisoners, who were from very different backgrounds and from different parts of the country, there was an opportunity for bonding and a sense of community: 'There was a foundation of principles among people'.

I usually term Robben Island the university of the world where I majored in humanities! The extreme oppression and level of sadism displayed by the white warders revealed them to be a very different breed from white people I had known at university and in society. They appeared as if they came from somewhere else.

Much has been written about this. Suffice to say I had never imagined, let alone experienced, the level of suffering that was deliberately inflicted by human beings on other human beings. There were no visits from family while I was on Robben Island. I was allowed one letter every six months. That was my only means of communication with family during my incarceration. For me there was also a deep and inner struggle. I found myself wrestling with God asking the question, 'How could a good God allow so much suffering in my country and now on this island?' It was in the course of that wrestling with God that I suddenly found inner peace, as if God had laid his hand on me. It was in a prison cell that I felt the call of God to serve him in the ordained ministry.

I have often been asked about what held us together amidst such pain and suffering. It was the bonding that occurs when men and women find themselves together in distress and the knowledge they had to survive together. It was the indomitable human spirit which enables us to overcome even the most horrendous conditions; a time when the spirit is stronger than the human body. I recall one incident, working in the searing heat, being shouted at to push our wheelbarrows still faster and harder while we struggled barefoot with heavy loads, all the while being beaten; one young man got to a point where he had enough. I vividly remember how he suddenly put down his wheelbarrow and shouted: 'We will die for our country!' At that time our spirits soared, even though we knew that we faced overwhelming odds as prisoners.

Although the desire of the prison authorities was to break our spirit and make us live to regret the ideals and dreams we had, nevertheless, the Spirit of the Living God enabled us to keep our heads high. That same Spirit developed in us an unshakeable faith in the God of Freedom, the God of Justice, the God of Hope who had touched our world of sad oppression with God's healing breath. I also recall how we would join together, night after night, in the singing of *Nkosi Sikelel' I Africa* (God Bless Africa). How that irritated the guards, and how that song of hope and freedom and glory echoed through the walls, across the sea into our beloved Africa. That sustained us and took us through the worst of the abuse to which we were subjected.

I was born in Kokstad, a small town in East-Griqualand where white, coloured and black people still lived side by side. My father was a parish priest for a black congregation (churches were segregated). We were a family of six, four girls and two boys. We are all alive at the time of writing. Mother celebrated her 86th birthday on 20 October 2001. My father was born on 8 September 1905. He died at the age of 82, four years before I was consecrated Bishop on 8 September 1991.

Working conditions for black priests were appalling, to put it mildly. Stipends were very low – approximately £36 per quarter – far less than the stipends of their white counterparts. My mother, who was a teacher, could not get a job because she was married. To supplement father's income, mother did some knitting and sewing. She also produced clothing for us in the same way. We were at times a laughing stock with our friends who came from homes whose parents had better pay packets than my father. Typically these were children of teachers, nurses and medical doctors. All black of course. No comparison with white counterparts whose salaries seemed enormous.

My father had cows which we milked and some ground where we ploughed and grew some vegetables to feed us. We were in some ways a self-sufficient family. By the grace of God, our parents managed to send us all to school and even to colleges of higher learning. We had to make do with meagre pocket money or none at all.

Housing for clergy, especially black clergy, was also appalling. Our home had two bedrooms, one for parents and the other for children. Some of us slept on the floor. When visitors came we had to abandon our bedroom and sleep under the kitchen table. Although visitors were most welcome in our home, nevertheless as children we resented them. When it rained, the roof leaked. We had to place buckets all around the house.

By contrast, the white priest who was my father's boss had a much more comfortable, even palatial house. Whenever we had to get communion wine and wafers which were kept in his house, we had to use the back door. For the greatest part of my father's ministry he used to ride horses on his visits to outstations – visits which would sometimes take up to three weeks. The weather conditions were sometimes terrible, with thunder storms, lightning and rising tides in rivers. Horses are also temperamental. One time father had such a bad fall that we thought he was going to die. I remember him inviting me to read morning and evening prayer with him at his bedside. I rather liked doing that. My father's boss of course had a car, and was not subjected to such a punishing schedule.

Years later my father hired cars and eventually bought a car for his visits to chapelries: needless to say the white authorities in the diocese called for a scrutiny of the books as it was not imagined that black priests could own cars. That incidentally had happened also when my grandfather who was also a priest bought a car. I recall driving with father in his visits and seeing the poverty and conditions under which people lived and worked in the farms around Kokstad.

When I look back over the unfair conditions which black clergy were required to work under I can see how unchristian they were. And yet I also understand that in the circumstances of the time, most people could not see this. We are prisoners of our backgrounds. But once a person has come to know what the conditions are, that person must do something by showing contrition and making amends. In the Church of the Province of Southern

Africa today clergy are paid equally and work under equal conditions regardless of their race.

The divide nowadays is more between those who are in what we call 'plum' parishes, i.e. the wealthy congregations, and those who serve in struggling rural parishes and dioceses or city parishes. There is an urgent need for radical improvement of clergy packages. Incidentally, I made this plea in the 1980s, saying that the Church in the year 2000 and beyond must rethink its employment patterns as well as the remuneration of its employees. This of course fell on deaf ears. Ironically, at the same time I also called for the Church to prepare for a time when apartheid would be no more. I was shouted down as a dreamer who did not know what he was talking about. Look at what has happened!

There were discussions at home about the situation in the Church which was oppressive for blacks which of course was a reflection of what was happening in the wider society.

My father and grandfather did not have the opportunity for their voices to be heard in the courts of the Church as debates were dominated by the colonial types, and procedures at synods were patterned on the Westminster model which can be very daunting and intimidating. Besides, they were not as cheeky and daring as the black clergy of my generation. However, I recall an incident that was organized by my grandfather. In 1943 an elective assembly was being held to choose a bishop and a black candidate had been nominated, among others (South Africa was not to have its first black bishop until twenty years later). At diocesan events white people were expected to be first to receive Holy Communion. But on this occasion, at St John's Cathedral, Umtata, my grandfather and his colleagues organized blacks to be first to receive communion. This caused quite a stir. When asked about his actions, he said he was led by the Holy Spirit! Incidentally, my grandfather gave me the name Njongonkulu. 'Njongo' literally means 'aim'; 'nkulu' means 'big'. So he had high hopes for his grandson!

One serious friendship that evolved was with Chris Hani whom I met in 1954 when I began studies for the Junior Certificate. Chris Hani rose to prominence within the ranks of the African National Congress and was later to become a key player in the formation of the new democracy. Tragically he was assassinated just before the first democratic elections in 1994.

In 1956 we both went to Lovedale High School, a boarding school, for our Senior Certificate studies. Afterwards we parted company as he went to Fort Hare University while I went to Cape Town. Chris was a very brilliant, quiet guy. He was a devout Roman Catholic. He used to top our class and I used to come trailing behind him. Perhaps that is why we kept close contact. At

7

Lovedale I also rubbed shoulders with Thabo Mbeki who became President of South Africa in 1999.

Lovedale was situated in Alice in the Eastern Cape. At that time it, together with Fort Hare and Healdtown, was considered a centre of learning – a kind of Oxford of South Africa. At Lovedale we had leanings towards the ANC Youth League. We used to cross the Thyume River to Fort Hare to listen to live debates by our seniors. I think that is where I began to be politically sensitized. My mind was opened further to real issues when I was in Cape Town University in the late fifties. Fellow students like Fikile Bam (who is now a judge), Archie Mafeje and others contributed to my political awakening. The independence of Africa and leaders like Kwame Nkrumah, Mnandi Azikiwe, Patrice Lumumba and others influenced my thinking at that stage. The subsequent arrest of Chris Hani and his decision to go into exile had an impact on me.

Apartheid damaged sport in South Africa in that black players were not eligible for selection for national teams: yet during my High School days at Lovedale we had such outstanding players, players who could have made an integrated national side. In fact we had such talent that if someone was picked for a game, he could not be sure of his place for the following match. It is going to take us some time, perhaps a generation or so, for sport in South Africa to become fully representative. When I retire from my present position which is still far into the future and if I have any energy left, I would spend time helping this to happen.

As the son of a priest I was not aware of any particular pressures. I was a boy growing among other boys, treated like other children. But while I was brought up in a Christian home, the last thing I wanted was to become a priest, because of the conditions under which priests served in those days.

I think that it was later, in my grappling with the question of God, and my anger as to why God allowed such suffering – when we understood ourselves to be a just cause for the liberation of humanity but here we were in the worst situations – that I would suddenly experience a stillness of mind. Then I felt in me a vocation to serve God in the ministry of reconciliation, perhaps in the ordained ministry.

Yet at this time I wanted to make big bucks. I wanted to be a commercial lawyer. That is why I registered for a B.Com.Law degree at the University of Cape Town. My father's resources were meagre and we struggled with the payment of fees. Luckily I managed to win a bursary for clergy children. This was not substantial but it did help.

I did not do at all well academically at UCT. I can attribute that to the environment that was prevailing at the time – political awareness and the conditions we lived under in Langa, one of the black townships in Cape Town. The main characteristic of townships is a lack of basic facilities such as electricity. The living conditions are very deprived and overcrowded conditions are not conducive for reflection as there is no space. That was and still is the plight of many black students.

By contrast, when years later I went to King's College, London, I did reasonably well. It was a different kind of environment. In fact, that was the first time in my life I felt recognized as a human being. More about that later.

After my release in August 1966 from the three-year term in jail, I had a two-year banning order which confined me to two magisterial districts. I had to report at the police station once a month. I was not allowed to mix with more than three people at the same time, which made it very difficult for me to go to church. I had to seek permission to attend church and to go to work. I managed to get a job as a labourer in a construction company. At first I became almost doubtful about my calling, suspecting for a time that it might have been the product of 'emotion'. But, after three years, I was unshakeable in my conviction. I went to see my father – because he was my rector, in Gugulethu, then – to say: 'I think I have a call to the ministry'. My father was very pleased, and immediately made an appointment to see the Archbishop, Robert Selby Taylor. And I remember coming to this very office where I now reside, and Selby Taylor turning to me and saying: 'I have been waiting for you.'

In January 1971 I was sent to St Peter's College, which was a constituent college of the Federal Theological College in Alice. The Fedsem as we called it had a very interesting history and made a unique contribution in the formation of ordinands.

Fedsem came into existence as a result of pressure from the Nationalist Party government which was determined to implement its apartheid policy. Hitherto, the various denominations that constituted Fedsem had their candidates for ministry prepared separately in their own respective colleges: the Anglicans at St Peter's, Rosettenville, the Methodists and Presbyterians at Fort Hare University, and the Congregationalists at Adams College in Natal. The apartheid government put pressure on the various Churches to close these places of training.

One of the major reasons for the attacks by the apartheid government against the churches was because of their ethos in education and the high quality of the products of their education. Most if not all black leaders in all sectors of society in present-day South Africa are products of church schools that were systematically closed by the apartheid government. The philosophy of apartheid policy in education was to produce blacks who would not aspire to the green pastures that were reserved for whites.

9

The measure that probably caused the greatest harm to future generations of black South Africans was the Bantu Education Act, introduced by Dr Verwoerd as Minister of Native Affairs in 1953, which deliberately condemned black children to an inferior education.

In opening the debate in parliament Verwoerd said:

Racial relations cannot improve if the wrong type of education is given to Natives. They cannot improve if the result of Native education is the creation of frustrated people who as a result of the education they receive have expectations in life which circumstances in South Africa do not allow to be fulfilled immediately. It simply creates people who are trained for professions not open to them. When there are people who have received a form of cultural training which strengthens their desire for the white-collar occupations to such an extent that there are more such people than openings available therefore good racial relations are spoiled when the correct education is not given.

(Suzman 1994)

Bantu education was henceforth under state control and grants were removed from the mission schools which had provided a good education for many blacks. Future generations of black children were to be relegated to the status of drawers of water and hewers of wood. Verwoerd went on to say:

What is the use of teaching the Bantu child mathematics when it cannot use it in practice ? What is the use of subjecting a Native child to a curriculum which in the first instance is traditionally European? I just want to remind honourable members that if the Native inside South Africa today in any kind of school in existence is being taught to expect that he will live his adult life under a policy of equal rights he is making a big mistake.

By an act of God's grace a site was found in Alice next to the University of Fort Hare where these denominations could work together in the formation of their ministers. Each college was autonomous and students lived, ate and slept within their respective colleges. However, all lectures (except denominational courses) were taken together. Being at Fedsem was one of the most creative periods of my formation.

The establishment of Fedsem was 'an act of hope, an act of faith, and an act of charity' – words used by Archbishop Joost de Blank on the occasion of the opening of Fedsem. Faith in God is what bonded the churches together in this venture. Never before in the history of the Church in Southern Africa had it ever been conceived that several denominations with differing doctrines and forms of worship would co-operate with one another, least of all in a venture such as the training of future ministers. This brought about hope for realizing our dreams for a united church in Southern Africa.

Dr E. Lynn Cragg, one-time doyen of theologians, had this hopeful comment to make during Fedsem's early days: 'In the ecumenical sphere, the seminary holds out great promise for the future. Not only will it draw together in a common life and service staff and students working there, but as they disperse through the land one may hope that this influence will spread.' Words of hope and prophecy, for the influence of Fedsem's students was soon felt throughout the land. In fact the majority of people in leadership positions in the Church in Southern Africa at the moment are former students of Fedsem. This augurs well for ecumenical co-operation.

Fedsem was a candle of hope in the arena of theological education during the period. It was a unique experiment in ecumenism that produced some of the finest black church leaders of our time. Fedsem was a sign of hope for the black people. It trained ministers who sought to relate theology to the needs and situations of their people in the context in which they lived. It was one of the institutions in the country that provided higher education of good quality to blacks. Further, the community of Fedsem comprised people of different racial and language groups, with different cultures and backgrounds. Because they were such a heterogeneous community, the amount of experience and insights gained from one another was immeasurable. Many visiting dignitaries from various parts of the world described Fedsem as an oasis in a country that was torn apart by apartheid policies that emphasized division along racial lines.

The University of Fort Hare had now been transformed from its former glory into an apartheid institution. The struggles and the tensions between the students and the authorities paradoxically made it the centre of the development of the philosophy of black consciousness. Fedsem's proximity to it ensured that a corresponding black theology was evolving. As a consequence, a generation of black leaders emerged in church and society who were able to carry the black community of South Africa through the traumatic era of the 1970s, the 1980s and the early 1990s.

I came to see that we owe our history to a colonial past and that our Church is steeped in a British/European ethos, and that a new understanding is necessary. A key date was 1995 when the Transformation Resolution was passed by the Provincial Synod of the Anglican Church in Southern Africa. This is the highest legislative body of the Church. The Transformation Commission which was then set up is a concrete form by which our Church seeks to transform itself into a truly authentic Church that has visibility in the communities it serves.

Foremost among people with whom we came into contact were those from the black consciousness movement under the leadership of Steve Bantu Biko. Biko was soon to be taken from us by a brutal political system that created people who performed reckless and murderous deeds in their endeavours to foist a European system on Africa. Biko brought to our society a simple message: there is hope in the midnight of despair. He sought to instil human values, such as respect for the other person, the need not to take advantage of the downtrodden, and for all to have a sound work ethic. At the heart of our humanity is a mutual interdependence.

Biko articulated the voice of black hope and aspiration in a forceful and lasting sense in those years. He gave a wonderful example of courage in the face of danger, and of dignity in the face of abuse. Although much was revealed by testimony before the Truth and Reconciliation Commission, I do not believe that we shall ever truly know the torment and torture that Steve Biko had to endure at the hands of the apartheid security police, or the stoic way in which he endured it until his death.

Fedsem prepared us for effective contextual ministry. I recall one incident when a visiting lecturer, the Revd Theo Kotze of the Methodist Church of Southern Africa, was addressing us on the subject of 'how to be non-violent in a violent world'. As we looked through the window we saw students from neighbouring Fort Hare being chased and beaten by police and they were heading towards Fedsem. One of my colleagues raised a point of order and said, 'Sir, look out of the window – let's go and put into practice what you have been teaching us.' So off we went and provided a buffer between the students and the police and told the police to leave Fedsem as it was private property. We won the day. It was this kind of witness that angered the government and later led to the expropriation of the Fedsem property.

It was a time when black political leaders were either incarcerated or in exile; young people were disappearing to be tortured, and dying under suspicious circumstances. The leadership that these people provided for the country had enabled the majority of South Africans to give expression to their legitimate aspirations, but it was becoming more and more difficult for them to be actively involved. Because of this, church leaders stepped into the breach and themselves became a thorn in the flesh of the government. A confrontation built up between government and church which, among other things, resulted in Fedsem being hounded from Alice, first to Umtata and then finally to Imbali. Regrettably, for various other reasons Fedsem was forced to close down.

I married Nosipho Ngcelwane in December 1972. It was a very happy relationship despite the fact that we were not blessed with children. After some

12

struggle as Nosipho had a couple of ectopic pregnancies, we decided to stop trying to have children. This was at my insistence as she ended up having to bear the pain which I could not take any more. Both Nosipho and I were deeply saddened by the fact that we could not have children of our own. We were traumatized by that. But together we worked through the problem and came to accept it. We took a positive view that after all there are so many children who need to be loved in this world. We saw our position as being set free to be available for God without having to give due consideration to family constraints.

After my ordination into the diaconate in December 1973, I was sent to the parish of St Mark's, Athlone, to serve my title. I was ordained priest on St Thomas' Day, 3 July 1974. My appointment to Athlone was breaking new ground. Never before had a black African served in a predominantly coloured parish. There were moments of joy as people in the parish readily welcomed me warmly and as we journeyed together on what was an experiment in cross-cultural appointments. There were also moments of tension as local government authorities showed hostility to this bold move by the Church. According to the Pass Laws that I referred to above, blacks had to obtain a permit for work. So I was not issued with one as I worked in what was termed a 'coloured group area'. But I defied them by going on with my job, as I believed that I must obey God rather than men. The parish was behind me in that decision.

There were also some lighter moments when for instance I did my house visits. I recall knocking on the door in one home and a child came and shouted back to her mother: 'Mummy, there is a milkman at the door.' Milk deliveries in that area were done by black men. Years later when I was elected Archbishop, one newspaper had a caption: 'Milkman of Athlone becomes Archbishop'.

After a brief curacy at St Mark's, Athlone, I was awarded a place at King's College, London to further my studies in theology. After a four-year period of study I obtained a Bachelor of Divinity degree, Associateship of King's College and Master of Theology. During that period I served as honorary curate at St Mark's, Mitcham, St Peter's, Hammersmith and St Mary the Virgin, Primrose Hill.

The period in London was a further learning curve for me in cross-cultural relationships. It was the first time I felt what it is to be treated as a human being with dignity and respect. It was the first time I could go to a live theatre and concert that were not designated for a specific racial group. My love for classical music, especially Mozart, developed during this period. I enjoyed watching rugby and I was a Welsh rugby supporter. My only regret is that it was never possible for me to set foot in Cardiff Arms Park, rugby's holy ground.

At King's College I majored in Christian Ethics under the supervision and guidance of the Revd Professor Gordon Dunstan. My Master of Theology dissertation was on the subject of the relationship between the notion of human rights and the Christian doctrine of man. The notion of human rights is about the rights that belong to a person simply by virtue of being a person. The biblical view of humanity states that human beings are created in God's image with dignity and worth. The canons of a human being's worth are generally held to entail that there are certain standards of human living that are universally recognized. But it so happens that in some areas these standards are not attained and that results in an affront to a person's dignity. The doctrine of human rights is an attempt by human beings at exercising their responsibility as God's stewards on earth in that it seeks to challenge all the injustices that distort the image of God in humanity. It is an attempt to establish a social condition where there are harmonious and peaceful relationships among the people of the world, and where people are able to realize their full potential as God created them. My study of this theme of human rights has greatly influenced my commitment to a just ordering of affairs in the world for the general well-being of all.

Towards the end of my studies at King's College while at the same time being an honorary curate at St Mary the Virgin, Primrose Hill, I was offered a parish by the Bishop of Edmonton. Some friends tried to encourage us to accept the offer out of concern about our well-being as political oppression was on the increase in South Africa.

I must confess that we found the offer very tempting indeed as we were enjoying being treated like human beings. We loathed the thought of going back to oppression, when we had attained freedom, appreciation and acceptance of our true humanity.

However, after much thought and prayer we turned down the offer. We thought about the needs of the Church in South Africa, and about the need to be in solidarity with the suffering and down-trodden people of South Africa. We thought that the least we could do would be to be a presence and a voice when occasion arose. We thought that those of us who had had such a wonderful experience outside the country, who knew that there was an alternative to apartheid and who had an option to return, should do so in order to be the leaven in society. We were glad that we made that decision and that God sustained us throughout.

Our Lord Jesus Christ says that anyone who would be his follower should take up his/her cross daily. No one seeks to carry the cross. It is thrust on us. Think of Mary, the Mother of our Lord; think of Simon of Cyrene. What happens in these cases is that God gives us the grace to endure. In all these things we come out triumphantly victorious through the power of him who loved us. (Romans 8.37).

Between London and Cape Town, I had a short spell as an assistant chaplain at St George's Church in Paris. That was another very exciting cross-cultural ministry. St George's served a very diverse English-speaking community in Paris – business people, the diplomatic corps, students, tourists and ordinary residents. St George's had an international flavour as people who joined us in worship every Sunday came from various parts of the world. We also enjoyed the cultural life that Paris offers. Before we knew, it was time to move on.

We arrived in Cape Town towards the end of December in 1979. We were offered the rectorship of the parish of St Nicholas, Matroosfontein. I was warmly received as the first black rector in a predominantly coloured parish. Coming back to South Africa we felt like birds that had been allowed to roam freely and spread their wings but which were now brought back into a cage. Apartheid's repression had intensified. I recall the protest movements of the 1980s in which two students were shot dead in front of our church. I was later to lead a funeral service that was attended by over ten thousand angry young people. That was a very tense situation. I approached that funeral service with fear and trembling. It's amazing how God takes over in situations such as these. One of the readings for the morning office that day was from Isaiah 52.1–12. The words of Isaiah in verse 12 – 'Yahweh will go in front of you, and the God of Israel will be your rearguard' – gave me strength to face the day in the assurance that God is with us. And indeed everything went very well.

After 18 months as a parish priest when things were going on very well for me and I was enjoying what I believe God had called me to do, I was invited by Archbishop Philip Russell to join his administration team and to be his representative in Johannesburg. Archbishop Philip was due to assume office as Archbishop of Cape Town on 1 September 1981 and wanted me to be part of his team. After much agonizing I accepted. In fact I had very little choice as Archbishop Philip was my boss.

My official title was Provincial Liaison Officer. My duties were as follows:

- representative of the Archbishop in Johannesburg;
- public relations officer for the Church of the Province of Southern Africa (CPSA);

- liaison with government departments and diplomatic corps situated in Pretoria;
- co-ordinator for the work of provincial departments;
- liaison with media and making statements on behalf of the CPSA in conjunction with the Archbishop;
- secretary of the publishing committee.

Johannesburg is the commercial capital for South Africa. At the time, it had the only international airport. The South African Council of Churches and other ecumenical churches had offices in Johannesburg and the CPSA's provincial departments were situated in Khotso House. That was why it was important for the Archbishop to have a presence there.

This was a very wide brief which made it possible for me to have an in-depth understanding of the workings of the CPSA. It was at this time that I was appointed to represent the CPSA at the Anglican Consultative Council and I served also on its Standing Committee. This meant that I also worked closely with Robert Runcie, Archbishop of Canterbury. This was yet another opportunity that enabled me to know more about the world-wide Anglican Communion. I count it a privilege and an honour to have worked very closely with three distinguished leaders in the Anglican Communion at the same time – Archbishop Philip Russell as his representative, Archbishop Desmond Tutu when he was General Secretary of the SACC, and Archbishop Robert Runcie as member of the ACC Standing Committee.

I was also privileged to be a member of two Anglican Communion peace initiatives. The one was when Desmond Tutu as General Secretary of the SACC was under investigation by the apartheid government through the Eloff Commission hearings. The Eloff Commission was set up by the apartheid government to investigate the South African Council of Churches. The government found the Council of Churches annoying because it stood for truth and justice and they feared Bishop Tutu's prophetic voice.

Archbishop Desmond Tutu's emergence as an outstanding leader in the midnight of apartheid in the 1970s was a source of encouragement and inspiration to many young black people. It gave us hope that there was a possibility of light at the end of the tunnel. I was privileged to work very closely with him in later years and eventually became his successor. His depth of spirituality and disciplined prayer life, sharp intellect, courageous leadership, love of people and commitment to justice and peace has left an indelible mark on me.

I recall being questioned by an official in the Department of Foreign Affairs when I was applying for visas for the Anglican delegation as to why the

Anglican Communion had an interest in these hearings as they were not contributing financially to the SACC. My response was that if you touch one bishop in the Anglican Communion you touch everyone in the communion with its 70 million worldwide membership. The testimony of representatives from the Anglican Communion, led by Paul Reeves, Primate of New Zealand (and later Governor of that country), had a significant influence on the outcome of the Eloff Commission's hearings, namely Desmond's acquittal.

Another initiative of which I am proud to have been a member was a visit to Namibia during the war. We spent seven days in the war zone ministering to a very traumatized people, ordinary people who were intimidated by the sophisticated military machinery of South Africa. It was both a physically and emotionally exhausting yet very rewarding experience. This was another testimony to the resilience of the human spirit. The team produced a report to the Archbishop of Canterbury. I was later privileged to testify on hearings on Namibia that were held at Capitol Hill in Washington prior to independence.

After three years as Provincial Liaison Officer, I was invited in 1985 by Archbishop Philip Russell to go and sort out some problems at St Bede's College, Umtata. This was one of our theological colleges that had been closed down through government interference. I was charged with the responsibility of re-opening it. It was during this period, while I was principal of the college, that my wife Nosipho died suddenly of a haemorrhage.

When Nosipho died, it was one of the darkest moments in my life. I found myself again asking questions, why would God take away my life partner at a time when we were doing the best for God at St Bede's Theological College? That in fact is one of the reasons why I decided I could not continue as principal after her death. We had gone into the ministry as a partnership, and this had been her wish all along.

It was another moment in my life when there was darkness. But God was again wonderful to me. He raised me up and I was able to face life anew. It was at that time that Archbishop Desmond Tutu invited me back to Cape Town to be the chief executive officer for the Church, a position I held for five years before being elected to be Bishop of Kimberley and Kuruman.

As Executive Officer I dealt with all matters relating to the synodical government of the church as well as all relating to its administration. One of my colleagues used to refer to me as canon bureaucrat.

In 1987 I married Nomahlubi Vokwana, a widow who had two children by her previous husband. So I had an instant family. Swazi and Vusi are now pursuing their careers after completing their studies at universities overseas. I do not think they have any inclinations towards ordination into the priesthood.

The last thing I ever wanted to be was a bishop. I had thought of going back to being a parish priest when I was elected to Kimberley and Kuruman. As Bishop of Kimberley and Kuruman I spent a lot of time travelling vast distances visiting clergy and people in that diocese. It is there I came face to face with the reality of poverty as found in women, children, the elderly and people with disability. It was there where I saw women spend four to five hours a day fetching water and firewood – where I saw in real terms the evil of apartheid with electricity pylons going over the houses of people to supply farms for white people, where I saw water supplies made available only to white farmers.

During this time as Bishop I was appointed onto the first Board of the South African Broadcasting Corporation after the democratic elections. One of the highlights of that time was being charged with the formation of a new religious broadcasting policy. This saw the opening of airwaves to faiths other than Christianity which had hitherto been the only religion allowed a public voice.

To my greatest astonishment and surprise I was elected Archbishop in June 1996 to succeed Archbishop Desmond Tutu. I used to say that I pitied the one who would succeed Archbishop Desmond. In my earlier days as Archbishop when the phone rang and people asked to speak to the Archbishop of Cape Town I would set off to find him. This was going to be a hard act to follow.

I was constantly being asked how it felt to succeed the famous Nobel Laureate. This was captured in a cartoon in one of our national papers. I was caricatured wearing a mitre falling over my eyes and ears and a sympathetic parishioner greeting me at the end of the service with the words 'Don't worry, Your Grace, it will fit in time'.

TWO

South Africa: the challenges

ADDRESSING INJUSTICE, LOCALLY AND GLOBALLY

South Africa has emerged from a baptism of fire. The miracle of transformation which saw a smooth transition from apartheid to democracy is a cause for great celebration and thanksgiving. It is a basis of hope for humanity about possibilities that exist under God for people to rise above their ideologies and personal agendas and be united by a common desire to seek what is good for the people and their country.

We now have in South Africa all the necessary instruments for a sustainable democracy such as a new Constitution, a Constitutional Court, a Commission for Human Rights, and a Public Protector as well as a Commission for Gender Equality. We are engaged in a process of nation-building which encompasses, among other things, major demands for reconciliation, reconstruction and development. This nation-building task also involves a precarious tension between working for good results which lie in the future and at the same time meeting the pent-up needs and expectations of people who for far too long have had to make do with far too little.

The Truth and Reconciliation Commission was one such instrument that was charged with the task of looking at our past with a view to setting up a process that will take us into a stable future in which reconciliation would be effected. However, its limited mandate and duration did not allow the Commission to dig deep enough into our past and come up with recommendations that would set the tone for lasting peace. There are still some substantial issues that need to be resolved, and chief among them is the whole question of reparations for victims of human rights violations.

Poverty and inequality

One of the greatest issues that is demanding our immediate attention is poverty and inequality. We inherited from apartheid a legacy of economic and social distress and dysfunction. As we heard from the National Poverty Hearings, organized by the South African Non-governmental Organisations Coalition in 1998, many go hungry every day, are exposed to disease, are illiterate, unemployed and homeless.

The deprivations around poverty are not just about low incomes; they include loss of human dignity: this is about human suffering. There is also poverty in terms of denial of access to opportunities for advancement. That is particularly telling since we live in a world in which, on the one hand, there are huge material and natural resources at our disposal, as well as dramatic technological advances, and yet, on the other hand, there are inequalities and uneven distribution of wealth resulting in the fearful consequences of poverty which we see in the faces of women, children, people with disabilities, the vulnerable, the elderly, migrants and refugees. The deprivation that poverty brings about also brings with it a retardation of knowledge, preventing all human beings from sharing in the increasing wealth of technological information that is available.

Many organizations in our country have signed a Declaration of War on Poverty: they include the Churches, the NGO sector, government, trade unions, the UN and, significantly, homeless people's organizations representing grassroots communities. The Declaration describes poverty and its effects, opening with words that are relevant to us all:

> The war on poverty and inequality is South Africa's most important priority and our greatest challenge. Eradicating poverty is essential to consolidate the gains of our new democracy. It is a precondition for social justice, peace and security in our land.

Those who subscribed to the Declaration have also prioritized some areas that require special attention. These include responding to the challenge of globalization, both its opportunities and dangers.

Necessary steps include finding solutions to unemployment and landlessness, increasing access to credit for the poor and encouraging small-scale production and entrepreneurship in the formal and informal sectors. The gap between high-income earners and low-paid workers must be addressed as well as the situation of the working poor. Children in situations of poverty, those with disabilities, older persons and other vulnerable groups need special attention.

The new Constitution has created an environment and a mechanism for the provision of 'full enjoyment of human rights'. The Bill of Rights makes provision for traditional civil and political rights, such as the right to equality, human dignity, freedom of association and of expression. It is unique in the world in its specific reference to the rights of access to housing, health care, food, water and social security, to an environment that is not harmful, to health and well-being and the right to basic education. These are fundamental rights that must never be viewed as secondary rights. They are an integral part of human rights that must be applied to everyone and protected by all.

The challenges

Our challenge is to turn the provisions in our Constitution into a reality, for we live in a society where there are great disparities between the rich and the poor. This is largely due to the hundred years of racially structured economic, political and social policies that were designed to benefit the white minority to the disadvantage of the majority of the rest of the citizens.

As Nelson Mandela said on the day of his release in February 1990:

> The white monopoly of political power must be ended and we need a fundamental restructuring of our political and economic systems to address the inequality of apartheid and to create a genuine democratic South Africa.

Political liberation has been realized. We now face the enormous challenge of restructuring the economy in such a manner that the well-being of all the citizens will be provided for. At the Poverty Summit in June 1998 Professor Francis Wilson said:

> What happened in 1994 was that the scaffolding of apartheid was destroyed but not the pillars. The pillars of land distribution remain, the pillars of inequality remain. What we have changed is the scaffolding which we created. We need to knock down those old structures and start recreating.

Our past was characterized by division, dispossession, exploitation, exclusion and injustice. To quote from Volume Five of the *Truth and Reconciliation Commission of South Africa Report*, section 38:

> The huge and widening gap between the rich and poor is a disturbing legacy of the past, which has not been reduced by the democratic process. It is morally reprehensible, politically dangerous and economically unsound to allow this to continue. Business has a particularly significant role to play in this regard.

Now we must strive for wholeness, inclusivity, fairness, equity and respect for the other person. Investment in human capital should be a priority. In the allocation of economic resources, priority should be given to the development of previously disadvantaged communities.

His Holiness Pope John Paul II called upon us in the new millennium to become heralds for human dignity. We need creative and imaginative minds to reform the economic system so that everyone has everything basic for human life. We need responsible stewardship, linked with equitable sharing of God-given gifts and resources, for the well-being of all. This is not only possible, but it is also a prerequisite for a stable future. We possess the resources and technology. All that is required is the political will and economic commitment. Political liberation must be converted into socio-economic liberation as well.

Setting targets for specific improvements is very helpful. Oxfam, for example, launched an initiative entitled 'Education Now' whose goal is to bring about basic education for all by 2015 – an effort to be applauded.

The Nobel economics laureate Professor Amartya Sen has emphasized that the validity of any economic policy should be judged on whether it takes into account the impact on people who are on the downside of the economy. He says that it is necessary to bring social deprivation into the domain of public discussion and create systems for social opportunities. This view finds support from Pope John Paul II when he says: 'We urgently need a new vision of global progress in solidarity which will include an overall and sustainable development of society.'

But sustainable development is being undermined continually by market failures, especially in the extremely turbulent global financial sector. Prospects for balanced growth and poverty eradication in countries ranging from Argentina to Zimbabwe have recently suffered enormous damage, thanks to international currency speculation, capital flight, the repayment of odious debt, stock market and securities manipulation, and other flows of finance that occur well away from any regulatory control system. Because the amounts of money are so vast and the present capacity of democratic governance so weak in comparison, it is worth a bit more reflection to learn from this sector's problems, and the problems it causes the rest of us.

Most importantly, perhaps, in the context of global financial instability and crisis, we need to assert that the market is *not* always right. Market forces have been shown not to be the panacea that market purists dream of. Morally neutral in themselves, unless they are controlled and directed their competitive nature leads to a situation in which the strong do better than the weak, the rich become richer and the poor poorer. The worth and dignity of people in human terms is irrelevant to the workings of market forces. Global financial instability and crisis have shown us that market forces can produce poor results for poor people. Market forces have no value base and produce a system which automatically supports the already rich. Market forces are oblivious to our humanness.

Now is the time, above all, to make the financial system democratic, transparent and accountable to the people, so that our own resources, as well as any other inflows of capital to our country, filter down to the people at the grassroots, who in turn feed it back into the economy.

Perpetuating the status quo, particularly where unequal access to economic resources has reached unprecedented levels and is among the worst in the world, cannot bring the much needed reconciliation, reconstruction and development in the new democratic South Africa. We must create models of hope and trust that will give the vast majority of people in our country a new chance. We have a responsibility to ensure that all people have the same opportunities to reach their full potential.

This is a *kairos* moment: we are in the early years of a new millennium in the history of humankind. The first Christians stood on the threshold of the first millennium in a state of hopelessness at the crucifixion of Christ. But God raised him from the dead: hence our age is one of hope, an age of new beginnings, an age of the resurrection faith. It is applicable to everyone, from the multinational corporations to the multinationals of the Church. The opportunity to start anew must be seized.

In this way the third millennium can be a Jubilee celebration and the Risen Lord can help us understand his proclamation, 'Behold, I make all things new!' and challenge us to join him in bringing new life and new hope to a new South Africa.

One place we may start is by addressing globalization, beginning with the international financial power that is inevitably used as the excuse for our debilitating failure to solve the most pressing socio-economic crises.

HOW THE INTERNATIONAL FINANCIAL SYSTEM IS STRANGLING AFRICA

The United Nations reports that the average African household today consumes 20 per cent less than it did 25 years ago. Even in relatively wealthy South Africa, our own per capita Gross Domestic Product has fallen over that same period, leaving us at the same level we were in the early 1960s, yet with far worse inequality than even at that time – the very zenith of apartheid.

What are the direct relationships between Africa's ongoing socio-economic tragedies and globalization? Africa has been 'marginalized' in the world economy, even as our continent has been drawn further into international markets. Aside from cultural and media domination by the West, our marginalization has occurred in the three main areas of economics: international investment, trade and finance. The problems of the financial system are especially acute and deserve our full concentration, but the other damaging effects of globalization should also be mentioned.

First, foreign direct investments – especially of fixed capital like plant, equipment and machinery, in sectors that can potentially develop and industrialize our continent – have not been forthcoming. The investment we receive is usually exploitative and extractive, concentrating above all on unprocessed raw materials. There are a few counter-examples, such as light manufacturing, textiles and car parts, yet major initiatives such as smelters are being built because our artificially cheap electricity can turn minerals into base metal products. Global warming, and the need to spread electrification to all who do not have it, are not properly factored in.

Second, in the area of trade, all African countries have tried to expand exports – at the behest of the IMF and the World Bank. We have done so even when it has required a diversion of resources away from our own people's needs. Our reward is ever-declining commodity prices, which today rest at levels lower than at any time since the Great Depression of the 1930s.

Africa has many problems, which naturally should not all be blamed on our involvement in the global market. But to the extent that the international economic system is implicated in our crises, we have an obligation to draw this to the world's attention so that we ensure those who are responsible change course.

Consider the example of Rwanda. The worst case of genocide in recent times – the death of nearly a million Rwandese in 1994 – was partly a result of the poverty entrenched by the structural adjustment policies imposed from Washington. This is according to research by the University of Ottawa economist Michel Chossudovsky, who was a government consultant after the tragedy.

Professor Chossudovsky has documented, in his book *The Globalization of Poverty*, how structural adjustment wreaked havoc after Rwanda suffered a 50-per-cent decline in export earnings during the late 1980s, when global coffee prices collapsed. The World Bank and IMF then began imposing the Washington Consensus programme, instead of adjusting the country's debt burden to compensate for lost export earnings. The programme included a 50-per-cent devaluation of the currency and the termination of agricultural subsidies, especially price supports to peasant coffee-growers. This, in turn, led to the desperate uprooting of 300,000 coffee plants. The subsequent privatization of the power and telephone utilities caused prices to soar. The Bank and Fund also imposed increased user-fees for public health services, and mass lay-offs of teachers, health workers and other civil servants followed.

Rwanda's foreign debt rose by more than a third during the early 1990s. Increasing amounts of incoming money – including World Bank 'quick disbursing loans' – were channelled into the purchase of military hardware from Egypt, South Africa and Eastern Europe. The size of the Rwandan army increased from 5,000 to 40,000. Because of monocrop dependency and a price shock – immediately worsened by cruel austerity programmes designed in Washington – and with international financial resources flowing into the weapons of war, there was economic breakdown. It is against this backdrop that we must consider the horrific ethnic strife that followed.

Likewise, other major problems faced by African countries – corruption by elites, environmental degradation, HIV and AIDS – have all been exacerbated by structural adjustment programmes. We hear from James Wolfensohn, President of the World Bank, that HIV and AIDS is now of concern to the World Bank. If this were really true, the loans it is offering to purchase drugs would become grants. The orders to privatize public health systems would stop and the cost recovery requirements, which have lowered health system utilization rates, would be reversed.

Support would be given to countries like South Africa, which has in the past discussed alternatives to buying anti-AIDS drugs from multinational corporations. These corporations continue to use patent protections to ensure high prices, even though five million South Africans are HIV positive and will die early because the drugs are unaffordable. Such alternatives include importing generic drugs from Brazil or India, or even setting up generic drug-production facilities in South Africa. A South African law allowing these solutions was severely attacked by the US government in 1998–99 and, although some gains have been made by the campaign to obtain drugs at lower prices since the pharmaceutical corporations had withdrawn a lawsuit against South Africa in 2001, the situation is not yet finally settled.

None of Africa's vast problems can be solved overnight. But we firmly believe that in the area of international financial relations, some very strong remedies can be applied immediately with the potential for extremely good results.

International financial damage to Africa

The problems Africa faces in our international financial relations include:

  (i) extremely high levels of debt for which there is very little to show, thanks to debt management which helps the lenders and hurts the poor;

(ii) the power of international lenders in imposing a development agenda on Africa that conflicts with our needs; and

(iii) the rapid flows of speculative hot money in and out of Africa that can, and do, diminish the value of our currencies practically overnight.

Western banks in the 1970s were flooded with liquidity as a result of the huge increase in the oil price by the OPEC countries which were seeking investments for their profits. The banks encouraged developing countries to borrow beyond their means. Large loans at the then small interest rates were taken out with the hope of producing economic 'take-off'. The billions of dollars of foreign debt that were initially contracted – in many cases by unrepresentative, undemocratic regimes which owed their power to Cold War machinations – very quickly became unrepayable. The debt was used to support unpopular governments in many cases. Most top-down development projects also failed, with even the World Bank's internal 'Wapenhans Task Force' acknowledging, for example, that 40 per cent of water supply and sanitation projects in Africa during the 1980s had 'major problems'.

But paying for the projects became increasingly expensive. Interest rates rose to historically unprecedented levels around 1980, compared to the previous decade when inflation-adjusted rates were actually negative. As a result, when debts were rescheduled, our countries repaid interest on past interest due! Such usury, which is often declared illegal in banking laws, including our own in South Africa, follows directly from the intervention of the IMF and World Bank. Both gave new loans to African countries to bail out the commercial banks' ill-advised old loans.

The repayment obligation has been brutal for Africa, averaging 16 per cent of government spending during the 1980s, as compared to 12 per cent on education, 10 per cent on defence and 4 per cent on health. In 1996, sub-Saharan Africa paid the developed world US$13.4 billion, in part by borrowing dollars in new funds and using US$2.6 billion of its Northern aid. By way of contrast, the cost of meeting basic goals in Africa for universal health, nutrition, education and family planning is only about US$9 billion a year.

In human terms, there is convincing documentation that women and vulnerable children, the elderly and disabled people are the main victims of debt repayment pressure. They are expected to survive with less social subsidy, with more pressure on the fabric of the family during economic crisis, and with HIV and AIDS closely correlated to structural adjustment.

The IMF and World Bank should have helped spread the cost of the bad loans by imposing lender liability. That is, they should have taken steps to punish bank support for very bad governments like the apartheid regime in

Pretoria. Many North American banks should have written off the loans made to dictators when subsequent democratic regimes emerged. They didn't, except as an accounting exercise which did not diminish African loan repayments.

As the Canadian NGO Probe International eloquently argues, these 'odious debts' should be repudiated. Indeed, there is currently a grassroots movement growing in South Africa demanding reparations on odious debts that were previously repaid, beginning with the World Bank's loans to promote expansion of the electricity system only for whites during the 1950s and 1960s.

What about the debt relief under discussion in official circles?

Unfortunately, under the Heavily Indebted Poor Countries (HIPC) initiative, debt relief – with strings attached – sometimes makes matters worse. This we learn from the case of Mozambique, as documented by the journalist Joseph Hanlon. By way of background, first the Rhodesian army and then the apartheid regime in Pretoria sponsored a vicious army, Renamo, which launched a civil war that killed an estimated one million rural Mozambicans during the 1980s. When peace finally arrived in 1991, Mozambique borrowed to pay for the damage done by apartheid's proxy army. The debt rose to more than US$5 billion, and Mozambique was so weak that it became a pilot programme for HIPC in 1996. However, creditors don't seem able to write off sufficient debt to bring the poorest country in the world to a sustainable level. The Jubilee 2000 campaign believed that the World Bank's definition of debt sustainability for Mozambique is too high. When Germany was given substantial debt relief by the Allies after World War II, she was treated far more generously than she herself is now treating Mozambique. Such actions remind one of the Parable of the Unforgiving Servant. Germany was expected to use only 5 per cent of the income she earned from exports to repay her debts. Mozambique will have to repay nearly 20 per cent of its export earnings in servicing its debt. Double standards are being applied – one for the industrialized countries of the north, like post-war Germany, and one for the developing countries of the south, like post-war Mozambique. This is not good enough.

At least the World Bank has set a new level of debt sustainability for Mozambique. But the governments of the G8, now including Russia, cannot agree to bring debt down to that level by offering sufficient debt relief.

The most important point here is that HIPC allows merely a write-off of unserviceable debt, which no one ever expects the poorest countries to repay in any case. But the strings attached for even negligible relief are extraordinary. In 1998, when the relief began to flow, it amounted to only a small proportion of what might have been expected. Conditions included an order signed by the World Bank President, James Wolfensohn, in March 1998 to raise the user-fees for public health services by a factor of five, and to privatize municipal water so as to impose what he already acknowledged were 'sharp' increases in water prices.

In June 1999, under pressure from protests at the Cologne G8 meetings, a little more debt was relieved. But Mozambique still spends far more in debt servicing than on health and education. Washington's expanded Mozambican debt relief in 1999 also entailed 71 brand new conditions. Among these, Mozambique must not resurrect its cashew processing industry using traditional industrial policy tools. It must also end state attempts to provide water to the rural poor. Moreover, the IMF also insists that parliament adjusts the overall tax structure to make it more regressive. As a result the rich will pay a smaller share of their income than they do now.

Even after massive flooding hit Mozambique in 2000–01, the World Bank and IMF refused to cancel any further debt, but instead simply offered new loans and extended the terms of repayment. This is the terrible fate of a country which finds itself listed among the world's poorest, with income per person around US$100 per year, and which follows World Bank and IMF quite loyally.

The degradation of democracy

A second concern about international finance in Africa is the loss of economic and social sovereignty, and the degradation of democracy. Even if we do not see the fingerprints of World Bank or IMF staff on all the policies that do us harm, we know that the pressure from international development agencies and private financiers does influence politics and policies.

What have been the effects of the Bretton Woods Washington Consensus policies on Africa? Budget cuts depressed our economies' effective demand, especially the buying power of low-income consumers, and led to declining growth. The cuts often affect the poorest, least organized groups in society.

Imposition of user fees led to a decline in utilization rates for health and educational services and, again, women, children and the elderly suffered disproportionately. Young girls are the first to drop out when school fees rise. When they cannot afford clinic fees, people get even sicker from preventable diseases, and then die earlier or are forced into hospital for expensive curative care. The so-called 'exemptions' for the poor rarely work due to administrative problems, corruption, or lack of publicity.

Recent cases where the Bretton Woods cost-recovery policy has been lethal are documented in a US congressional report. They include a rate of Gambian malarial insecticide usage five times lower under the policy than it had been under a free programme. There was a 52-per-cent reduction in outpatient visits in Kenyan health centres once fees were applied. On the other hand, Malawian primary school enrolment increased from 1.9 million to 2.9 million (mostly represented by girls) once school fees and uniform require-ments were abandoned.

In the course of promoting privatization, World Bank and IMF economists failed to determine how state agencies could supply services that enhanced 'public goods'. For example, such public goods include the positive effects of water supply on public health, environmental protection, local economic activity and gender equality. Thus all state services were reduced to mere com-modities, requiring full cost-recovery and elimination of subsidies.

When interest rates jumped to very high levels once financial controls were released, or when a foreign currency crisis emerged, small and medium-sized businesses were often wiped out. Likewise, the lifting of price controls along with foreign currency liberalization and currency devaluation generated severe inflation in many countries, alongside a surge of luxury-goods imports for elite urban shoppers.

Inability to control the flow of money

A third area of international financial domination of Africa relates to our in-ability to control inflows and outflows of money. In terms of inflows, the few African countries which have managed to attract portfolio investments – usually stock and bond market assets bought temporarily by New York or London investment houses – were shocked at their destructive power.

In Zimbabwe, a panic attack by international investors in November 1997 led to a 74-per-cent crash of the Zimbabwe dollar in just four hours. Many of Zimbabwe's economic problems stem from the vulnerability that followed the failed 1991–95 structural adjustment programme.

Post-apartheid South Africa has had three major runs on the currency. The first was in February 1996 after a rumour that President Mandela was sick. The second was in June 1998, in the middle of the East Asian crisis. The third run occurred during 2000–01, as the rand fell from R6 to US$1 to R13.8 to US$1 at its lowest point. There are many debates about whether the cause was contagion from other crises (Argentina, Zimbabwe), capital flight by the major firms who are sending profits and dividends to their new London financial headquarters, or blatant currency speculation by inter-national banks and local firms.

Part of the problem is indeed an ethical dilemma about how to correct past economic injustice. Wealthy individuals have taken the opportunity of financial liberalization to spirit wealth out of Africa. In South Africa, the people who financially benefited most from apartheid are those who have been most delighted that, under pressure, the post-apartheid government has gradually relaxed its exchange controls beginning in 1995.

Towards an African peoples' consensus

African scholars and civil society activists realized these problems from very early on. The United Nations Economic Commission on Africa, led by Adebayo Adedeji, offered the African Alternative Framework to Structural Adjustment Programmes in 1989. Although Adedeji was very persuasive in his call for inward-oriented development that first and foremost meets our citizens' basic needs, we who work at the grassroots level had not caught up with the early criticisms of Washington. In various forums, the logic of the Washington Consensus was regularly contested by our continent's leading economists, including Samir Amin, Fantu Cheru, Thandika Mkandawire, Guy Mhone and Dani Nabudere. Many oppose the single-minded pursuit of balanced budgets, because – as John Maynard Keynes established during the 1930s – state budget deficits may be necessary when the private sector is stagnant.

Likewise, social scientists increasingly oppose the cost-recovery philosophy imposed by Washington. Instead, they promote a human-rights-based culture, through which all our citizens' most basic needs will be met, regardless of whether they can afford the fees. Similarly, they continue, privatization of essential services must stop so that our service agencies are able to take advantage of public and merit goods (such as public health improvements that come from free water). Because there is no profit motive, private companies have no interest in promoting these benefits or services, so typically people lose their access when they cannot afford to pay, even though the cost to society can be enormous.

Even more fundamentally, we should have more national-level control of our own economies, especially the power to set interest rates, tariffs and taxes according to our local needs and not according to the premium demanded by international financiers. To this end, taxes on international financial flows are certainly a good idea – to 'put sand in the wheels' of speculators, as the late Nobel economics laureate James Tobin described his objective.

We also learn from Africa's progressive economists that subsidies, price controls, exchange controls and import controls are potentially very valuable tools of industrial and social policy. They can help assure that basic consumption needs are met, that resources are not allowed to flee our countries to offshore banking centres where they do no good, and that hedonistic consumption of luxury goods by elites does not take priority over essential living requirements. Likewise, it is our responsibility to stop 'hot money' from flowing into our domestic stock and bond markets, given the increase in economic vulnerability that comes from such speculative funding. It may also be our intention to demand higher taxes in countries where this is feasible, so as to achieve redistribution from the wealthy to the impoverished. At the same time, we need to reorient our savings systems, so they no longer support unproductive stock market speculation and luxury real estate developments.

And if to do these things we must release ourselves from debt peonage – by demanding the repudiation and cancellation of debt – we will campaign to that end. And if the World Bank and International Monetary Fund continue to stand in the way of social progress, movements like Jubilee South Africa will have no regrets about calling for their abolition. To that end, the World Bank Bonds Boycott movement is gaining even greater momentum. Even a money centre city like San Francisco decided to redirect funds away from Bank bonds into other investments, on the moral grounds that taking profits from World Bank operations contributes to poverty, misery and ecological degradation. More and more investors are realizing that profiting from poverty through World Bank bonds is not only immoral, but will not make good financial sense as the market shrinks.

To those who say that Africa desperately needs a World Bank or IMF loan because we cannot access international capital markets, our economists are replying, 'So what? That's fine by us.'

What Africa needs is not more hard currency: US-dollar-denominated loans for rural education, to use one example. Such projects can be paid for with local currency and do not require any dollar-denominated imports. Why, then, should Africa take dollar-denominated loans which are often mainly used by African central banks to pay back immoral debt and to import luxury goods? When we need basic imports from abroad, what would be most helpful is a reformed export credit agency so that trade finance is available. Reformed export credit agencies should lend on cheaper terms and be increasingly accountable; this is something for which citizens, workers and environmentalists have been campaigning.

Africans are more confidently expanding the critique of the existing financial system, and offering alternatives along precisely these lines. Activists are also engaged in direct demonstrations at the IMF and World Bank offices. In Lusaka and Nairobi, for example, women's groups organizing such protests in 2000 faced arrest and harassment, but persevered. In addition, communities in Chad, Cameroon, Lesotho and Namibia have strenuously objected to large World Bank-designed projects such as pipelines and dams in their countries. Workers in Nigeria and South Africa have periodically downed tools en masse in protest at Washington Consensus policies. In 2000, the Nigerian protests forced Lawrence Summers, the US Treasury Secretary, to leave the Lagos meeting a day early.

A month earlier, four million South African workers sacrificed a day's pay to make their statement. Subsequently, protests in Prague, in the Czech Republic, were echoed in Cape Town, in Johannesburg, in Durban and in East London, where Jubilee South Africa and other social movements called for the World Bank to leave Pretoria. These calls have continued to reverberate, and the protests against corporate globalization will not die down until transformational changes are made.

African consciousness of the damage done by the international financial system is at an all-time high. This is in no small part because many of the world's churches have helped to spread the word about the Jubilee campaign. In a globalizing world we need transparent and accountable international instruments that embody equity and fairness and espouse the common good of all human beings. Ending the domination of an unjust global financial system may require the most radical surgery that we have ever seen. As examples, we are regularly campaigning to restore exchange controls, to impose a Tobin Tax on international financial transactions and to re-establish controls over our own internal financial resources. We continue to insist upon cancellation of all outstanding Third World debt, and even, as the International People's Tribunal on Debt recommended in April 2002, closing down the IMF and World Bank, so as to release the pressure that their economists' boots place upon our necks.

At the end of the day, this is, after all, about power: the power of international financiers and allied bureaucrats, versus the power of people.

POVERTY – THE NEW APARTHEID

Julius Nyerere, a president of Tanzania, said in his address to the Maryknoll Sisters in New York in 1970 that 'poverty is not the real problem of the modern world. For we have the knowledge and resources which could enable us to overcome poverty. The real problem, the thing which creates misery, wars and hatred among men, is the division of mankind into rich and poor.' The same is true in South Africa. There are so many destitute people amidst plenty. One only has to drive through the northern suburbs of Johannesburg to Alexandra Township to see that this situation exists.

A British government study (Department for International Development, 1997) revealed that more than 800 million people in the world are hungry, and the number may well exceed one billion by the year 2020. Many more are malnourished. The world's population of underweight children below five years of age is expected to grow from 193 million in 1997 to 200 million by 2020, with most of the deterioration in Africa.

World Bank studies show that people living on less than two US dollars per day number almost half the world's population. The least developed countries have grown in number from 25 in 1971 to 48 this year – 33 of those are in Africa. The number of poor people in Latin America and sub-Saharan Africa is expected to rise.

Every year 8 million children die of diseases linked to impure water and air pollution; 50 million children are mentally and physically damaged due to poor nutrition, and 130 million children – 80 per cent of them girls – are denied the opportunity to go to school. All this in a world in which 20 per cent of the population enjoys 80 per cent of the world's wealth.

In 1998 I was privileged to be one of the co-chairpersons of the National Poverty Hearings – an initiative of the South African NGOs, the Human Rights Commission and the Commission on Gender Equality. We heard up to 16 oral submissions each day of the hearings, held in all nine provinces over several weeks.

During these hearings I came into contact with a people of hope and of dignity. Listening to people's stories of survival amidst squalor and deprivation gave me a sense of the resilience of the human spirit. Like the boy of 12 who looked after his 7-year-old brother. They had no home and nothing to eat. They used dogs to sniff out food in a rubbish dump. The older boy always made sure that his young brother had enough to eat before helping himself. Luckily one day they were found by a woman who took them home, scrubbed them clean, gave them food and took them to a shelter. Here is a modern version of the Good Samaritan. This story, however, epitomizes the story of many others that we heard.

They spoke with the same voice. 'We do not want handouts. We do not want charity. We have brains. We have hands. So give us the skills; give us the resources; give us the capacity to work out our own existence in order that we might have dignity, that we may be fully human.'

One of the dangers we face in the new, liberated South Africa, is that we may continue to embrace values that do not encourage one to speak up for the poor. Political parties are proud to say that they speak for different interest groups in society, but they are not always keen to speak of fairness, equity and justice for the poor. We live in a world in which our media, particularly television, reinforce the view that money and riches should be worshipped. It is a world in which money enjoys more powerful rights than human rights. Only among the faith communities does there seem to be any will to challenge Mammon, the god of riches.

It is well known how poverty impacts on a nation's health. It affects every facet of our lives and is, I believe, a reflection of an iniquity as insidious and diabolical as apartheid: insidious because it is not seen in the stark terms of racial discrimination; diabolical because those with power and wealth often refuse to recognize the inequities imposed on the poor.

What has South Africa achieved as a nation?

The fundamental restructuring which President Mandela asked for on the day of his release has not realized the hopes and dreams of the majority of the people of South Africa.

In the years subsequent to the inauguration of the new government positive things have happened: for example, houses have been built, primary health-care clinics have been set up for poor communities, other positive actions have been taken. Unfortunately we cannot say the same on the economic front. The government's macro-economic policy, which we all hoped would bring in economic changes and, therefore, the enhancement of the quality of life for all South Africans, has not materialized. The government's drastic plan as set out in the Growth, Employment and Redistribution (GEAR) document has failed to reach anywhere near its targets.

The plan was to create jobs and grow the economy in order to bring about economic justice and to eradicate poverty. What has happened in these two vitally important areas?

Job creation:
- GEAR planned to create 126,000 new jobs in 1996 for example. In fact they lost 70,000. This represents a net loss of 196,000 jobs in 1996.
- Likewise in 1997 they planned to create 252,000 new jobs. In fact they lost 142,000 jobs. A net loss therefore of 394,000 jobs.
- If we add these losses together, then in just two years we lost 590,000 jobs. This is not economic justice!

Economic growth:
- The drastic plan was to have economic growth in 1997 of 2.9 per cent. What actually happened was that it grew by a mere 1.7 per cent.
- The plan for 1998 was economic growth of 3.8 per cent. We achieved only 0.1 per cent.

34

While I welcome President Mbeki's reference to positive signs of growth in the economy, I am dubious of the rosy picture he paints. I am not the only one who doubts that the government's present economic policy is taking us anywhere fast. A Zapiro cartoon in the South African *Sunday Times* of 13 February 2000 showed a huge, fat goose with the name 'Economy'. On the barn door nearby is a notice which reads 'Golden Egg due 1996'. 1996 has been crossed out and replaced with 1997 which has been crossed out in turn and replaced with 1998 and so on up to 2000. At the egg end of the goose is President Thabo Mbeki – pipe in mouth – bending forward and waiting with keen interest. At the head of the goose – in farmer's dungarees – stands Trevor Manuel, the Minister of Finance. Mr Manuel is saying 'It grows fatter and fatter but it just won't *lay!*' And, just outside the barn door, the poor wait in vain.

I have been reading Clem Sunter's latest book entitled, *Never Mind the Millennium. What about the next 24 hours?* He gives a frightening statistic that 93 per cent of school leavers in South Africa currently cannot find work in the formal sector of the economy.

Clem tells us that technology has created a world permanently in surplus. If this is so our lives should be ruled by the economics of surplus, not by the economics of scarcity. This is a total contradiction of predictions that there wouldn't be sufficient food to feed an over-populated world. Today we have a surplus of just about any commodity including cotton, oil, gold, steel, copper, nickel, aluminium and coal. Even if the entire production capacity of North American cars were wiped out overnight, there would still be a surplus capacity.

It may surprise you that Clem Sunter – a highly regarded economist and futurist – tells us that poor people aren't poor because of the scarcity of resources and products. They are poor because they are denied the opportunity to make money for themselves.

He and others talk about Britain and its '30–30–40 society'. This is the catch phrase to describe the 30 per cent of people who will never be employed and need to be taken into account for strategic planning. Then there is the 30 per cent who are employed but in insecure and largely informal jobs. Only 40 per cent are in safe and permanent employment. To quote Clem Sunter: 'If 60 per cent of Britons are permanently excluded from secure employment, one shudders to think what that percentage is in this country!'

I feel especially for the Eastern Cape. It is the second largest province in the country, and has the highest unemployment rate in the country. Of those who do work – blacks and whites – three-quarters earn less than R2,500 a month. Half earn less than R1,000. More than half the people

35

still fetch water from a distance. In the rural areas women spend four to five hours a day fetching water and firewood. Rural women are also subjected to authority structures that place tremendous restraints on their development. Thirty-four per cent of people in the Eastern Cape use pit latrines and an additional 30 per cent have no toilet facilities at all. The health implications are horrendous.

Diseases which affect the poor

Another significant challenge that is before us is finding suitable vaccines for the diseases that, largely, affect the poor – such as HIV and AIDS, malaria and tuberculosis.

In 1997, 20.8 million out of the 30.6 million people living with HIV and AIDS were in sub-Saharan Africa. It is likely to be 36 million by now. South Africa, Namibia, Angola and Zimbabwe are the countries in which the numbers of affected people are growing the fastest. The age group 15–24 is the group most affected, and it is said that one out of every five schoolgirls in South Africa is infected. Of those infected 79 per cent are heterosexual, 13 per cent are babies and 1 per cent are infected by blood products. By 2010 the life expectancy of South African women will be 37 years. Fifty per cent of people alive today will reach the age of 60. In 10 years' time we will have two million AIDS orphans in South Africa.

A United Nations AIDS report stated that already 13 million people had died in Africa from this disease. Women are five to six times more likely to get AIDS than men are. The reasons for this are many and include both physiological and socio-economic factors. For example, many women lack the power to insist on contraception, and many women are raped or abused – in and out of family relationships. Rural women especially have limited access to health care, and so on. Age also plays a role in that girls are more susceptible to infection and are also sexually active (with or without their consent) at a younger age than boys are. Older men often prefer younger women and so on.

Malaria kills more than one million people a year and perhaps as many as 2.5 million. The disease is so heavily concentrated in the poorest tropical countries and overwhelmingly in sub-Saharan Africa, that nobody even bothers to keep an accurate count of clinical corpses or deaths. Tuberculosis is still taking the lives of more than two million poor people a year and, like malaria and AIDS, would probably be susceptible to a vaccine, if anyone cared to invest in the effort.

In an article in *The Economist* of August 1999, Jeffrey Sachs, the noted

University of Columbia economist, says that the basic problem is that 'global science is directed by the rich countries and for rich-country markets, even to the extent of mobilizing much of the scientific potential of the poorer countries'. He goes on to say that private investors and scientists doubt that malaria research will be rewarded financially. Creativity is needed to bridge the huge gulf between human needs, scientific effort and market returns.

Jeffrey Sachs makes four proposals:

1 Rich and poor need to learn to talk together and develop a common plan of action.
2 Rich and poor countries should direct their urgent attention to the mobilization of science and technology for poor-country problems. To this end he proposed the creation of a Millennium Vaccine Fund which guaranteed future markets for malaria, tuberculosis and AIDS vaccines.
3 The global regime on intellectual property rights needs to be revised. At present so-called 'first world' institutions and international corporations are busy taking out patents on every new intellectual idea and discovery possible. The poor are being excluded once again, and will continue to be so unless some sense of global responsibility is introduced. The ongoing debate over access to AIDS medication in this country is an indication of this. Incentives for innovations which will benefit the whole of humanity – not just the rich – must be provided with no more delay. This is the global responsibility of all those in power.
4 There needs to be a serious discussion about long-term finances for the international public goods necessary for the heavily indebted poor countries to break through to prosperity.

I think we all accept that it is time for radical and decisive steps to address the issues I have raised – which threaten our future survival.

New economic systems

More and more frequently, leading economists (for example, the Nobel Prize winner Joseph Stiglitz) are recognizing that the Washington Consensus – which provides the framework for international financial systems – is flawed. What is needed is for us to put into place new economic systems: economic systems which put people, not profits, first. All the more tragic then, with the collapse of communism, that the free-enterprise capitalists have jumped on the bandwagon of excessive profit and rampant greed. The failure of communism does not make unrestrained capitalism right. Communism arose in the first place because of the injustices within capitalism.

When His Holiness Pope John Paul II met the International Jubilee 2000 delegation in September 1998 he said:

> The law of profit alone cannot be applied to that which is essential for the fight against hunger, disease and poverty. The Catholic Church ... has consistently taught that there is a 'social mortgage' on all private property, a concept which today must also be applied to 'intellectual property' and to 'knowledge'.

The Holy Father is right. The law of profit – it has already been proved – cannot put food in the bellies of the millions of mothers, fathers, children, grandparents, workers – the millions who hunger and starve, here on the African continent, in Latin America and in Asia. The law of profit will not allow them the drugs they need to treat the most stressful and appalling diseases known to humanity: HIV and AIDS, malaria, hepatitis and tuberculosis. The law of profit will not help the majority in the world to climb out of the deep well of poverty into which they have been plunged by a ruthless economic system whose main driving force is profit and greed. That is why we need new economic systems – economic systems which place human values at their centre, not monetary values.

Jesus Christ came to challenge and enable us to take responsibility for our lives, to use our power to make choices. We do not have to be enslaved by the elemental forces of nature and economic systems, we can be liberated. This requires discipline and control. With discipline and control we can overcome the scourge of abject poverty. With our God-given responsibility, we can use the resources God has given us for the good of one another and his world. God has provided for our need, not our greed.

In the very first chapter of the Bible, in the book of Genesis, we hear God telling us to look after and care for this world. This does not mean, as many have interpreted it, selfishly exploiting it. In being given 'rule', we are to look after, nurture and care for what God has given us so that this world will be a better place for us and for our children. There is a saying which should always be in the forefront of our minds that 'we have not inherited this world from our parents, we have borrowed it from our children.'

To sustain the world we need a new brand of science and technology, which should be governed by a new brand of economics and politics, with a sound moral foundation. Ethics should precede politics, economics and the law because political action is concerned with values and choices. Ethics must, therefore, inform and inspire political leadership to fulfil our obligations as human beings for the well-being of others.

The inequalities of the world are increasing at an alarming rate. The rich are getting far too rich and the poor are becoming desperately poorer. God looks down and does not like what he sees happening on earth. The Jewish Old Testament prophets called long ago for justice and righteousness in our dealings with one another and our care of God's created order. We must demand action. If the rich and the powerful do not take action, they, with the rest of the world, will suffer.

A CALL TO RELIEVE POVERTY

A plea to the rich nations

My first call is to the rich nations, and the multinational corporations, who must recognize that they cannot continue on the present course of economic growth and exploitation which disregards the consequences upon fellow human beings and the natural world. The rich must recognize that the purpose of life is not the acquisition and accumulation of wealth but the development of the world for the good of its inhabitants and the world itself for future generations. This change of attitude has enormous repercussions. We must grasp the responsibilities given to us to care for the future of our people and of our world.

While we allow the injustices to continue, social unrest will increase, drug trafficking and political turmoil will be the order of the day, while the natural world becomes a barren wasteland, less and less able to support the demand humans place on it.

If, on the other hand, we set out resolutely to establish justice for our world, sharing its resources, the future is one of peace and harmony. The choice is before us today. As we read in the book of Deuteronomy (chapter 8), the choice is ours: to follow God and his commandments wherein we are then promised prosperity and life; or to follow the false god of today which is Mammon.

We cannot allow those who wield economic power to govern the world on the criteria of economic profitability only. We have to consider the well-being of people and the natural world and recognize the responsibility we have for every facet of our lives.

We have to take responsibility for our world, for our economic system – harnessing it to serve us, rather than allowing it to enslave us – and for one another. We need a fundamental reappraisal of economics, so that need and capacity, rather than supply and demand, provide our guidelines.

Life is a challenge to realize our sovereignty, and the responsibility that goes with it. To quote Professor Klaus Nurnberger from the University of Natal:

> Economics is too important to be left to the economists, politics to the politicians and matters of faith to the theologians. Responsibility for the economic and ecological wellbeing of humankind rests with the entire academic community, in fact, with the citizenry at large.... A humanity which has lost its sense of responsibility has abandoned its birthright.
>
> (Nurnberger 1999)

As we cast our eyes into the future we would do well to remember the words of UNICEF:

> The progress of nations will be judged not by their military or economic strength, nor by the splendour of their capital cities and public buildings, but
>
> - by the well-being of their peoples;
> - by their levels of health, nutrition and education;
> - by their opportunities to earn a fair reward for their labours;
> - by their ability to participate in decisions that affect their lives;
> - by the respect that is shown for their political and civil liberties;
> - by the provision that is made for those who are vulnerable and disadvantaged; and
> - by the protection that is afforded to the growing minds and bodies of their children.

A call to Christians and the Church

My second call is to the Christians who have a clear biblical imperative to place poverty high on our agenda. We all know the passage from Matthew 25.41–6, where Our Lord tells us that whoever has fed the hungry has done this to him. Again in James 2 we are warned that faith without works is of little value. In Africa, we have a further cultural imperative in the concept of *ubuntu*, under which we have an obligation to uphold each other's dignity and to ensure that all have what is needed to live a fully human life.

In 1985 a Church of England report, *Faith in the City*, stated categorically that poverty was not just about the shortage of money. It is also about rights and relationships, about how people are treated and how they regard themselves; about powerlessness, exclusion and loss of dignity. But the lack of adequate income, and the ongoing syndrome of the haves and the have-nots lie at the root of all these problems.

In their book in which they examine this report, D. B. Forrester and D. Skene note:

> Questions of distribution – what is distributed, to whom and in what way – are of importance to the Christian tradition because they raise major spiritual issues. As the Russian theologian Berdyaev, said 'Bread for myself is a material matter, but bread for my neighbour is a spiritual matter'. Any pattern of distribution expresses some understanding of the dignity and worth of the human individual, and must be measured against the Christian belief in the infinite value of each person and the equality of all before God.
> (Forrester and Skene 1988)

The first thing to recognize is that poverty requires a holistic approach. Many of our churches have 'development desks', and have a vision that goes beyond relief work to address the root causes of poverty. But if humanity is going to measure any degree of success in this battle, everyone – religious institutions, business, the state and civil society – is going to have to join hands to come up with a comprehensive approach which clearly spells out short- and long-term objectives and strategies by which to implement them. One the one hand, we need to give urgent attention to soup kitchens and feeding schemes by which the poor will be able to survive, but on the other hand we need a long-term view which will inextricably bind human development with economic growth and the sharing of resources.

The influential church leaders' Forum of South Africa some years ago established an Ecumenical Commission on Poverty. Some of its tasks include:

- to raise awareness of the issue of poverty in our congregations and among our people;
- to study the issue and raise questions about what needs to be done;
- to encourage initiatives, projects and funds;
- to stimulate giving among our own people in terms of caring for each other;
- to encourage a culture of compassion, giving and caring.

But as Christians, we need to go far beyond talking about poverty. The Methodist Bishop Mvume Dandala has suggested that as churches we adopt a programme based on the idea of sacrificing a meal a week so that everyone has a meal a day. Between the Church Unity Commission and its observer Churches, we claim a church membership of nearly nine million people. If only half of those nine million people sacrificed one meal a week and contributed what they would have spent to relief and development, we would be looking at vastly more resources with which to make a significant impact on the effects of poverty in our land.

Not only that, but churches would be in a far stronger position to lobby various stakeholders, particularly business, to play their part in the battle against poverty, for we would be able to present our challenges with integrity, having shown our willingness to put our money where our mouths are.

A call to businesses

My third proposal is addressed to businesses. Much of the debt which is crippling our country is owed to the country's financial institutions. So my suggestion is that business seriously considers heeding the jubilee call to cancel this debt that is owed it by the people of South Africa. This would free massive resources to be ploughed into communities in the form of development.

Further, it would command huge respect internationally. In the successful transition to a negotiated settlement on apartheid, South Africa claimed and occupied the moral high ground, becoming a beacon of light and hope. Business has an opportunity to become a further example of a new sense of community and sharing.

I am fully aware of the complexities entailed in financial transactions, but I have tremendous confidence in our captains of business and industry, many of whom are active members of our churches. Their institutions have done sterling work in the past, and indeed continue to do so, in the fields of social responsibility policies, empowering programmes, and the present policy of unbundling large corporations. In the Anglican Church we are investigating ways of establishing contact with leading business people, to pursue this vision further.

A call to government

My fourth word is directed to the South African government. It faces a mammoth task of addressing the imbalances inherited from the past, and its commitment to the task that is confronting it is admirable. But too often one hears of funds that should have been spent on reconstruction, but which are apparently lying unspent in the state coffers. The temptation to ignore issues of poverty is great, since the poor are generally not among those in our society who command respect and who wield power. But just as I am convinced that we have people of tremendous calibre in business, so I am equally convinced that we have among the ranks of government committed Christians and others who have heard the rallying call to address poverty, and who will be prepared to take the necessary action to eradicate it.

A CLEAN SLATE: AFRICA'S SPRINGBOARD TO NEW HOPE

In the 1960s many African countries emerged from protracted freedom struggles against colonial oppressors and had to find their own feet economically. They grasped at economic lifelines thrown out by developed countries. But the lifelines were flawed. The leaders of these countries incurred massive debt on behalf of their people – people who were unaware that they were being dragged into the mire of foreign debt that would lead them further into a sea of poverty. From the 1960s onwards the world's economy was dramatically reshaped as rich nations lent money to the poor.

The tragedy is that the people of these poor nations had no understanding of the debt they were incurring, or of its long-term consequences, any more than ordinary people of developed countries understand the intricacies of the world economy. The result is that millions of people in developing countries now live in poverty, while a massive transfer of wealth from the people of the south takes place to the developed and industrialized nations of the north.

Quoting figures supplied by the World Bank, Jubilee 2000 Coalition's report notes that Africa owes US$227.2 billion to creditors – nearly $400 for every person in Africa. These debts are more, sometimes much more, than what most Africans earn annually. Put into perspective, they are only twice as much as the short-term debt owed by South Korea, and a much smaller proportion of the $3 trillion the United States owes the rest of the world. But while Africa's debt may be small in global financial terms, it remains a tremendous burden for the continent – particularly for countries that have a history of exploitation by colonial powers. World Bank figures illustrate that in 1996 Africa transferred $14.5 billion of its precious resources to OECD (Organization for Economic Cooperation and Development) countries. This equals the amount spent in Africa on education, and twice the amount spent on health.

In 1996, the countries of sub-Saharan Africa paid their creditors more in debt service than they received in loans. For every dollar Africans receive in aid from developed countries, they repay $1.30 in debt service. In other words, the money is on a perpetual merry-go-round. It is not used for development. The poor do not benefit. Charity is not charity at all.

Contrary to general assumptions therefore, the rich are not paying the poor. The poor are paying the rich. These enormous debts, and the way in

43

which they divert money and resources from other more productive development in Africa, lead to unhealthy relationships of dependency between African governments and their creditors.

In a frank admission at the G7 summit in Naples in 1994, the then French President, François Mitterand, conceded that 'despite the considerable sums spent on bilateral and multilateral aid, the flow of capital from Africa towards the industrial countries is greater than the flow of capital from the industrial countries to the developing countries'.

His comments are the more striking when one notes that a wealthy country, such as Britain, refuses to repay debts much larger than those of many poor countries. A report by the Jubilee 2000 Coalition points out that Britain still owes US$12.8 billion to the United States for loans made during World War II; the rest of Europe owes $17 billion. None is repaying the debt. The morality of such countries insisting on debt repayment, when they are themselves defaulting, must thus be seriously questioned – particularly when it is the poor who suffer.

South Africa has a debt which is the legacy of apartheid. This legacy can be more readily understood when it is appreciated that in 1989 the debt stood at only R80 billion (US$16 billion). By 1995 the debt had increased astronomically to R263 billion ($51 billion), and now stands at R309 billion ($62 billion). The repayment of this debt is the second highest item in the country's budget, after education. Consequently, it has been extremely difficult for the new democratic government of South Africa to embark more vigorously on necessary human development and social improvement programmes in order to redress the imbalances that it inherited from the apartheid regime.

South Africa's debt has three components:

- The first is international debt. It is estimated to stand at some 5 per cent of the total debt, which is small compared to the size of the debts of its neighbours. This portion of the debt ought to be cancelled outright as apartheid was declared by the United Nations as a crime against humanity.
- The second component, estimated at some 40 per cent of its debt, is of a public nature, owed to the Public Investment Commission, a non-profit institution that funds the pensions of civil servants. Possibilities exist for the restructuring of this debt in a way in which it would not adversely affect the civil service pensions. For instance, the South African NGO Coalition (Sangoco) has estimated that such rescheduling would reduce South Africa's debt by between R15 billion to R20 billion (US$3 billion

to $4 billion). This needs creative fine tuning by those with expertise in this field, as well as the political will to address this issue.

● The third part of the debt is owed to local commercial institutions within South Africa itself, such as Sanlam and Old Mutual. Some believe that there are mechanisms available that could be applied by these huge financial institutions, which should be explored so that this burden of the debt can be alleviated without adversely affecting policy holders. The result could be a solution that would benefit everyone, not least the companies themselves. The necessity for long-term economic growth and stability, together with pure logic and enlightened self-interest, should provide sufficient reason to do so. South Africa's recent history shows that such business institutions have considerable inventive resources to share.

How can the creditors respond?

John Young and Aaron Sachs, in *The Next Efficiency Revolution: Creating a sustainable materials economy*, write:

> An all-out effort is needed to find creative solutions to the debt crisis, and tariff and trade agreements need to be modified in such a way that countries can become more self-sufficient and maximise the value they add locally to the materials they do produce and export. Such new policies will also generate more economic spinoffs – related economic development – than do current policies, which largely prop up 'enclave' industries that are more closely connected to processing firms in other countries than to local economies. Money also needs to be devoted to retraining and education for workers in those industries that are forced to reduce employment, with an eye to shifting those workers to sectors that will grow as a result of the changes underway.

This is the type of new thinking that is needed – thinking that has in mind the development of people and their own, local economies, for the benefit of the largest number of people. Creative solutions such as those envisaged by Young and Sachs are sorely needed in a country such as South Africa. They are desperately required in the developing countries of the world in general, and Africa in particular.

In respect of the former frontline states, as they were known in the 1980s, many of them suffered as a result of the policy of destabilization in the southern African region. Countries such as Angola, Lesotho, Mozambique,

Malawi, Zimbabwe, Zambia and Tanzania were among those that experienced such hardship.

These countries, together with others like Namibia, Swaziland and Botswana, found themselves in the midst of the struggle between different world forces, with southern Africa as the battleground – forces backing on the one hand the status quo in South Africa, and on the other, the liberation movements. Their debts incurred during this time should also be declared odious and written off. This would lead to a combined saving for them of almost US$38 billion.

South Africa has already written off the debt of Namibia. Other countries should do the same, thus restoring an element of equity.

An official of the World Bank who was quoted in the media recently is right when he says that the initiative that will see relief given to Mozambique 'is not about the debts of the past but our hope for . . . the future'. Every country and international agency involved in the debt debate should embrace these views so that we can see the developing world take a giant stride forward in economic terms. Jubilee 2000 seeks to address the imbalance in the economic affairs of the nations of the world. The debt bondage of the people of Africa has often been compared to the human bondage of slavery. It has been pointed out that in the course of the Atlantic trade in slavery, 24 million people were placed in servitude. More than one and a half million were thought to have died as they crossed the Atlantic Ocean.

The United Nations Development Programme has argued that today's debt bondage can directly account for the deaths of millions of children. In its 1997 Human Development Report, the UNDP says that if resources were diverted from debt service into health, clean water and sanitation, then the lives of 21 million children could be saved before the turn of the century.

Correcting these imbalances is not easy. But thankfully one *can* report on some successes. The initiative of the G8 to refinance and reschedule some of the debts of the poorest countries – the so-called Heavily Indebted Poor Countries initiative – is an historic recognition by these two institutions that something has to be done. Regrettably, the HIPC initiative, which began with great promise and was received with great enthusiasm, appears to be running out of steam (see p. 28).

Much more can be achieved with political will, as the British Minister Clare Short has acknowledged in respect of the eradication of poverty. But we also know that only public outrage in the countries of the developing world, as well as those of the G8 countries and developed economies, will ensure that all the world's indebted countries are given equitable treatment and freed from the bondage of debt.

In 2000 I raised with the Swiss government the issue of monies loaned by that country's banks to underpin apartheid. This was despite a UN declaration that the abhorrent political system was a sin against humanity. I hope that, instead of waiting the five long decades they did before reimbursing victims of Nazism, we may soon anticipate some kind of Southern African reparations fund for apartheid's victims. German, US and British banks are also being approached to account for the massive interest profits taken from South Africa at the additional social expense of the prolongation of apartheid.

The Meltzer Commission – set up by the US Congress to make proposals for the future shape of the Bretton Woods institutions – recommended complete debt cancellation. They recommended this not only for the bilateral lenders but also for the multilateral institutions led by the IMF and World Bank. This was unanimously agreed by the Commission and received widespread backing from, among others, the Director of the United Nations Conference on Trade and Development and the Secretary General of the UN, Kofi Annan.

Five actions need to be taken by the creditors:

1 Stop taking payments from the poorest countries immediately and ring-fence the money for the poor, to demonstrate their political commitment to cancelling debt and ensuring that money released is used to tackle poverty.
2 Commit to the cancellation of 100 per cent for the poorest countries from all creditors including multilateral institutions, particularly the World Bank and IMF.
3 Ensure that heavily indebted and impoverished countries excluded from the HIPC list – such as Nigeria and Haiti – become eligible for debt cancellation.
4 Set in process a new mechanism for dealing with debt and lending. This needs to be a fair and transparent process that helps to ensure that the debt crisis does not return in the new millennium.
5 Help indebted countries set in process a recovery plan. This could be along the lines of the Marshall Plan used for Germany after World War II. Southern Africa could be used as a pilot project.

What can Africa do?

Having cleaned the slate, Africa should brace itself to take its destiny into its own hands. It is time for the giant of Africa to wake up from its deep sleep and to take its rightful place in the world. We are a people and a continent with a rich heritage, the cradle of humanity.

Some 25 years ago, the doyen of pan-Africanism, Dr Kwame Nkrumah, made an impassioned plea: 'Africa must unite or perish.' This was in May 1963 when the Organization of African Unity (OAU) signed the Charter for Unity in Addis Ababa. One of the key tenets of the OAU's Charter remains as valid today as it was then – that African countries should 'co-ordinate and intensify their co-operation and efforts to achieve a better life for the peoples of Africa'.

In preparation for the millennium, representatives from 35 African countries gathered in Accra, with a mission to renew that ambition: 'To co-ordinate and intensify our co-operation and efforts to achieve a better life for the peoples of Africa.' We should pledge ourselves to work vigorously and earnestly in the first instance for the cancellation of the international debt which would give Africa an opportunity for a fresh start. This is in accordance with a biblical injunction of profound significance, not just to Christianity, but to humanity as a whole. The injunction is that periodically, every seventh sabbath year, we should review our social, political and property arrangements, and that every 50 years, the Jubilee year, we should right the wrongs that have been woven over the period into economic relationships, relationships between debtors and creditors, between the poor and the powerful.

Above all, 'we should sound the trumpet of Jubilee, and declare liberty throughout the land' – these are the words engraved on the Liberty Bell in Philadelphia, which inspired the revolutionaries who struggled and died for American independence from her own colonial power.

There are signs of a resurgence in Africa, as illustrated by the revival of the economies in several countries and a commitment to democracy. The first South African Nobel Peace Prize Laureate, Albert Luthuli, on receiving the award, said: 'In Africa, as our contribution to peace, we are resolved to end such evils as oppression, white supremacy, and racial discrimination, all of which are incompatible with world peace and security.' That has indeed happened in so far as white supremacy is concerned. We have to guard the fundamental human rights of people, which are sacrosanct. We must ensure that people are not taken advantage of because of their social or political standing in a mercenary world.

Now is the time for the countries of this continent to settle down to a period of sustained and invigorating growth – economic and social growth that will trigger development worldwide. It is most encouraging to note that a recent study by *The Economist*'s Intelligence Unit reckons that five of the world's 20 fastest growing economies are in Africa. That is remarkable and we need to build on this.

To do so, governments must recognize that with freedom comes responsibility. Thus, any freedom from debt must be accompanied by a commitment to ensure that people benefit from the advantages that will follow.

It is urgent that there be a meeting of minds of statespersons and other opinion-formers in Africa on the need to take the aspirations of Africans further. Political leaders should be looking beyond mere bilateral or regional economic agreements, to ambitious concordats, such as that which has seen the European Union flourish.

The concept of an Economic Union of African States needs urgent support backed by research to ensure that it will benefit the greatest number of people. Such a Union would co-ordinate economic activity in the continent of Africa for the general well-being of its people. It would ensure, *inter alia,* that:

- Africa would never again be marginalized, thereby becoming the begging bowl of the world;
- Africa's resources would never again be exploited;
- Africa would not become the dumping ground for environmentally repugnant refuse, such as nuclear waste; and
- conditions exist for attracting investment capital from all parts of the globe into the continent of Africa.

The Justice and Peace Department of the Southern African Catholic Bishops' Conference has said: 'The struggle for economic justice is the most profound and far-reaching of any of the great struggles that have been waged in human society. It is global, affects all sectors of society in all spheres, including business, labour, religion, politics and education. It is about women, youth, ecology and education, theology and the arts.'

An Economic Union of African States would bring us a giant step towards economic independence, and the opportunity to negotiate with more muscle and realistically with the developed and industrialized world. Africa has much to offer the world, but it must do so on an even basis, and not with the odds loaded against it. At the same time, much should be done to forge partnerships between like-minded institutions in civil society – not just in Africa, but worldwide.

Africa is a big place – a huge and wonderful place. Though we have lived with great sorrows and problems dragging at us, now we are holding in our hands the big, the tremendous promise of new life. It was from Africa that our species may have begun the settlement of the planet. But Africa holds something key not only to human origin but to the human present and future, to human fulfilment. That great African, Anton Lembede, was one of the first to articulate the concept of a universal harmony as emanating from Africa. It is a message that we would do well to reflect upon. Speaking of Africa long before any sub-Saharan African countries had obtained their independence, Lembede uttered these prophetic words:

> Each nation has its own peculiar contribution to make towards the general progress and welfare of all humankind. Man's great task is to shape, mould and render harmonious the elements or parts of the universe. Our great values, namely truth, goodness and beauty – themselves forms of harmony and ultimately one single harmony – are, as it were, beacons pointing for us the way to absolute harmony – GOD. It will only be when Africans are free that they will be able to exploit fully and to bring to fruition their divine talent and contribute something new towards the general welfare and prosperity of humankind.

Lembede and Nkrumah were way ahead of their time. Few took them seriously. The time has come for us to pay more attention to the great visionaries of our contemporary African heritage. Another great African visionary, Robert Mangaliso Sobukwe, put it this way: 'World civilization will not be complete until the African has made his contribution. And even as a dying, so-called Roman civilization received new life from the Barbarians, so will the decaying so-called western civilization find a new and purer life from Africa.'

There is something about the air of Africa, something mystical, yet obvious, something of the old but with the expectancy of discovery. It is time to move forward, and to share the healthy, invigorating air of Africa with a world that has grown fatigued with old values. Africa stands at a time where it can and must play a pivotal role in influencing the next millennium. And for that it must be freed from the last shackles of oppression that is holding it back – the yoke of international debt.

WHY THE REST OF THE WORLD SHOULD CARE

I am often asked to fly to another continent and speak about the situation in Africa, and the role which the rest of the world has in restoring Africa to wholeness after years of exploitation. When I have done this I board a plane and return home to familiar surroundings and local occupations. And my hearers will almost certainly become absorbed once more in their own present concerns. Five years later, I wouldn't blame them for having trouble remembering my complicated African name!

But it doesn't matter if they forget my name. They have heard not only a story of Africa, but a story of humanity.

Those I speak to, as educated women and men, stand on the shoulders of others. Boosted by generations of received knowledge, they can see into the distance. There's a wide world out there, and they are able to understand the experiences of Africans vicariously, not as their own first-hand encounters, but as human experience. And as citizens of the world, I hope that they can apply the knowledge for the benefit of humanity.

From the Western perspective, poverty and poor communication make some places seem far distant. The journalist Robert Kaplan writes about these 'cut-off' places, and calls them 'the ends of the earth'.

The practical fact is that Africa has little meaning for most who live in the northern hemisphere, particularly Americans. There is really no interest in Africa until some tragic situation is played up in the press such as the terrible flooding in Mozambique which made a million people homeless, and brought the threat of disease and death to thousands and misery to all.

But for us Africans our continent is the centre of the world. And for the rest of the global community, Africa really holds something central, something key. Kaplan suggests an exercise to clear the northern mind of its habitual orientation. Take a global map and turn it upside down. Put the North Pole at the bottom and settle Antarctica at the top. What happens? Europe and North America grow small and distant, while South America and Africa fill the eye (Fletcher and Mufson 2000).

What's happening in this huge swelling continent of Africa? The *Washington Post* pointed out that many things hang in the balance at the present time. 'Africa has never experienced more democracy or sustained economic growth than in recent history.' At the same time, one cannot ignore the epidemics of AIDS and other diseases which cut down working men and women, fathers and mothers of tens of millions of children. Neither can one ignore the grinding poverty, environmental deficits, civil wars and corrupt governments (Kaplan pp. 4–5).

What is happening today in Africa is that the continent is turning from a long, hard period in its history to a bright future. Increasingly the people are claiming their rights to the basic goods of humanity. Africans are becoming more determined to reject the sickness and poverty, the environmental degradation, the waste and destruction of irresponsible governments – and to realize the fullness of justice, peace and prosperity.

Let us apply these understandings in the area of human rights. Recognized as the most basic of common goods, human rights are often thought of universally, and conceived of in the abstract. But human rights are never personally encountered or truly understood in the abstract. Human rights, or their abuse, are always experienced in their particular details. The woman raped by police has a name, a husband, children. The young men, children even, who are conscripted into rebel armies are the hope of their parents, the companions of their friends. The little girl born into such poverty we can hardly imagine it – who has a life expectancy of perhaps five years during which brief time she will struggle against malnutrition and disease – is the beloved special child of God.

It is the specific, personal experience of human rights or their forfeit which grounds and validates any universal expression of human rights as a common good. So the particular human rights experiences of Africans are essential to any complete and valid universal understanding or defence of human rights.

I would like to talk about human rights in an African context as Africans struggle with them in three areas:

- the South African experience of apartheid;
- the unsupportable burden of foreign debt; and
- the growing recognition that the majority of Africans are coming from behind in a whole range of basic human freedoms, on which depend the simple fulfilment of human possibility, God's intentions for humanity.

Apartheid was founded on a principle that there are inherent differences between people according to their race classification. Consequently rights and privileges were granted to the white race on the grounds that it was superior. The fundamental plan of apartheid was to deny people their authentic humanity based on the colour of their skin and this determined every facet of life in apartheid South Africa.

This constituted a violation of fundamental human rights for the vast majority of South African citizens. The one distinctive feature of a human right is the simple fact that it is something a person possesses by virtue of one's nature as a human being created in God's image with dignity and worth. Something that belongs to all people everywhere regardless of status and position in life. As Professor J. E. S. Fawcett puts it: 'Human rights might be better called common rights for they are the rights and freedoms which do not depend for their exercise upon the holder belonging to any particular community group or category: they are the rights of all human beings' (Fawcett, 1979). Universality, therefore, is the main feature of a human right.

Human rights are so called because they are the kinds of rights that belong to human beings simply by virtue of their personhood. Nothing else considered. As Professor Maritain says:

The human person possesses rights because of the very fact that it is a person, a whole, a master of itself and of its acts and which is not merely a means to an end, but an end which must be treated as such. The dignity of

52

the human person signifies that, by virtue of natural law, the human person has the right to be respected, is the subject of rights, possesses rights. These are the things that are owed to [a person] because of the very fact of [being a person].

(Maritain, 1971)

That is why the United Nations declared apartheid a crime against humanity. Morally righteous people around the world mobilized themselves against apartheid until the granite wall collapsed.

I now turn to the massive problem of unpayable debt owed by the poorest countries in the world, most of them African, to developed-country lenders. Don't misunderstand: this is not primarily a financial problem. Although counted in dollars, the burden of foreign debt is a crisis for humanity. Vast sums of money are pouring out of impoverished African countries into the coffers of those in the so-called 'first world'. The direct result is that the impoverished country governments have wholly inadequate funds to address basic human needs for food, clean water, health and education. The debt crisis is a matter of life and death. African children, women and men are dying while old debts to wealthy lenders are being repaid. This is a human rights emergency!

Debts have accumulated over four decades, and they have become a monster. Poor, indebted countries are transferring their tiny wealth to rich countries. Interest payments mount to terrifying proportions, so that over time countries have repaid the amount of the principal many times over without retiring the loans. For every US$1 that rich countries lend to developing countries US$11 comes straight back in the form of repayment on debts owed to the rich countries. So wealth is not trickling down from the rich to the poor, as people like to think. Wealth is actually trickling up from the south to the north. Countries of the south find themselves giving away, virtually free, earnings from their precious commodities like coffee, copper, tea and sugar. Trickle-up, not trickle-down. This is a form of economics which denies us our humanity, rich and poor alike.

These two specific areas of human rights struggle – apartheid and debt – move us into the broader realm of human freedoms. I'm not talking only about the core human rights on which reasonable people agree – things like the right to be protected against unwarranted search and seizure, the right to fair trial, the right to live unmolested in one's own home and neighbourhood, the right to pursue a livelihood and own property. I'm talking about a whole cluster of human freedoms, which have been considered unaffordable or unnecessary for poor countries, by most northern economists and development 'experts'. Since these so-called experts are the ones who control the foreign loans on which poor countries have had to depend, their view has been decisive for the daily life of most Africans. Northern experts who insist on expansive human freedoms for themselves say that such freedoms are luxuries for poor countries.

The right to basic health care seems to be a luxury. Unfortunately rich countries and corporations see no material benefit to themselves from providing funds to research these epidemics adequately. They prefer to concentrate on the diseases of the well-off – those which promise profit to the manufacturers. Spiritual benefit which comes from helping greater humanity is not often seen as adequate reward.

Contrasting with the notion of human freedoms as luxury, we need an understanding that 'the human enterprise – the whole work of human fulfilment, human development – can only authentically be pursued as a process of expanding human freedoms.' These 'include elementary capabilities like being able to avoid such deprivations as starvation, undernourishment, escapable morbidity and premature mortality, as well as the freedoms that are associated with being literate and numerate, enjoying political participation and uncensored speech and so on' (Amartya Sen).

But I can tell you that equating development with money, evaluating the human condition only in coin, is a great untruth. Human development cannot be equated simply with income level. For poverty is not just about low incomes; it is about loss of dignity, being treated as nothing, and basic needs not being met.

Yet much of the world accepts as unavoidable, as a normal fact of life, so much human 'unfreedom' – Professor Sen's word – so many violations of human rights. Homeless orphan children scavenging in a dump is so sad – but what can one do? Occasionally moral outrage gathers around a human rights abuse which is too obvious to ignore. Thankfully, apartheid in South Africa was one of these. The intolerable burden of poorest countries' unpayable foreign debts is becoming another. But most of the time, human rights abuses don't concern any but the people suffering the abuse. The rest of the world sleeps soundly and rises in the morning to meet the demands of their own lives.

Humanity cannot, actually, be fragmented and disconnected one from another. We are all branches on the same family tree. When one branch withers, the rest of the tree is affected, at least under the skin. Another way to understand the essential interconnectedness of all human beings is to look to the Author of Life, to God, and to pay attention to what God teaches us about who we are.

The God I know and love is one God. Yet one of the great mysteries of the Divine is that contained within the Godhead are three distinct persons. We know God the Father, God the Son, and God the Holy Spirit. Three persons, eternally and inexpressibly united. As David A. Scott, William Mead Professor at the Protestant Episcopal Seminary in Virginia, puts it, 'God has a life: internally, essentially, God is in relationship.'

We know that all human beings are created by God, in the image of God. In this image, human beings are meant also to be essentially in relationship – in relationship with other human beings. To the degree we reject human relatedness, we shatter the image in which we are created. If there are children scavenging in a dump on the other side of the world and I ignore this, then the wholeness of my own being is deeply and essentially shattered. For human beings, it is impossible to say the other's life is not my concern. That is deeply untrue, and I deceive myself if I hold that view.

The inescapable conclusion to draw from this understanding of human nature is that all of us are affected by abuse of human rights and freedoms. All of us are responsible for the abuse. All of us are responsible for righting the wrong. This is a global responsibility for the global community.

I have focused on the African experience of human rights abuses and human 'unfreedom', because that is our particular story. And Africans have particular responsibility, for refusing to live under apartheid, for throwing off the burden of unpayable foreign debt, for determining that our societies shall honour the essential freedoms.

Towards the end of 1999, I addressed a South-South Summit of the worldwide Jubilee 2000 coalition, which brought together in Johannesburg workers for debt relief from Africa, Asia and South America. I emphasized the responsibility of developing countries to educate and mobilize our own citizens, and also to build a global consensus to transform the systems, which create 'unfreedoms'. We are working towards four objectives:

1 We are working for massive and immediate cancellation of the unpayable debts of the poorest countries of the world.
2 We are working for economic systems which put people, not profits, first.
3 We are working for economic systems based on respect for nature and the environment, for wildlife and plant life. Such economic systems are deeply embedded in traditional African culture and practice. Here especially, Africa has a unique and necessary contribution to make to the global project of human fulfilment.
4 We are working for democratic accountability and transparency. This

means building democracy at home, and at the same time throwing off the control which foreign lenders and investors exercise over our economies and over our governments.

We Africans are stepping up to our responsibility to bring in human rights, human freedom, across our continent.

And the rest of the world also has a responsibility. The northern hemisphere has a special responsibility. The prosperity of the countries of the developed world has not been earned by their citizens alone; must of it has been given to them by earlier generations; and much has been brought to them from their colonies and their relationships with the poorer parts of the world, often from unequal and exploitative relationships. They have been given much.

To whom much is given, from him, from her, much will be expected. The concept of human obligations

serves to balance the notions of freedom and responsibility: while rights relate more to freedom, obligations are associated with responsibility. Freedom and responsibility are, however, interdependent. Responsibility serves as a natural, voluntary check for freedom. In any society, freedom can never be exercised without limits. The more freedom we enjoy, the greater the responsibility we bear, towards others as well as ourselves. The more talents we possess, the bigger the responsibility we have to develop them to their fullest capacity. We must move away from the freedom of indifference towards the freedom of involvement.

(Inter Action Council)

Those of you reading this that are citizens of the northern hemisphere, among all the world's people, will have a voice which commands attention. You will have the ability to think and imagine, and the ability to articulate and persuade.

In the course of your life you command resources. You make personal decisions about consuming and investing the money you earn. And many of you will be business leaders, making greater decisions about finance and investment.

You exercise power – within private enterprise, within local or national or international government and public institution, within NGOs.

Each one of you will have a voice, resources and power, which the vast majority of people in the world only dimly imagine. For the sake of all of us, you have a particular responsibility to use your power for the common good. I urge you to seek, throughout your life, direct experience of different cultures and circumstances. Don't be content with an insulated existence. Expose yourself to the experiences of the world. The world's life is your life!

A NEW HUMANITY FOR A NEW AGE

Facing and working with AIDS

We live in a world that is often described as a global village wherein global realities have a significant impact on local communities. We have become very much aware of our interdependence and our mutual entanglement. To my African friends, I write as one who is in the struggle with you. I come to them as one who weeps over our dead, and yearns for a better life for those suffering illness and loss. I express my deepest appreciation to them, the carers of people living with – and regrettably dying from – HIV and AIDS. They are heroes whose vision and compassion extend beyond themselves to include all who are infected with or affected by AIDS. They deserve the gratitude of their nations, and the heartfelt thanks of their communities.

Without them and the efforts of their agencies and programmes there would be very little support for these who suffer so much. It has long been my strong conviction that no one should die alone. And because of carers and what their programmes do, no one is either living or dying alone. Without the people of God and what they bring to this pandemic, we cannot move forward as human beings. We all look to a time when this pandemic is but a sorrowful and painful memory. But until then, we have each other and our unquenchable hope and deep commitment to secure the future.

Disease and pandemics bring out the best and the worst in people. On a broader scale, it is also clear that a pandemic such as HIV and AIDS have devastating personal, social, political and economic consequences. Quite simply, no one comes to the HIV and AIDS pandemic from a place of neutrality. And because it is a disease which involves two basic biological facts of our lives, namely sex and death, there are always strong emotional responses.

Those who care for others with AIDS bring so much to us today. Not only their care and compassion, which is exemplary, but also their deeper understanding that even one death from AIDS is one death too many. They bring the sensitivity and insight that knows that, unless we work actively to prevent this disease, another generation will be born into the chaos of illness and death.

I know something of this kind of commitment. Today South Africa is free. For some South Africans a free South Africa is the way it has always been in memory. But it wasn't always this way. The generations of struggle and agony to win the right to be a nation for the majority, and not the minority, were often bitter and fraught with frightening losses and disaster. There was suffering in every segment of society. There was bitter discord and differing opinions about the way forward. The struggle for our freedom, as South Africans, and subsequent transition have been remarkable and painful. It is little wonder that, when reflecting on the AIDS pandemic, that Nelson Mandela declared AIDS the next struggle. South Africans' struggles were then and are now filled with challenges to our cultures and traditions, as well as to our way of thinking about the world. We must cling to a vision of hope and a future without AIDS.

When I was a prisoner on Robben Island, I would toil at the work I was ordered to do in the earnest hope that the whole world would become outraged at the government's injustice and become committed to our cause. I would pray in the prison, yearning for a better day. I would allow my mind to visualize a day when all the people of God in South Africa would select a president who represented the majority. All of us there would imagine a time when anyone in our society could travel freely across all boundaries into any neighbourhood, knowing that we belonged there and that no one would challenge our right to be there.

In those days, I would look over to Table Mountain and I would question in my heart if there would ever be a time when all would be free to think what we will, speak as we must and maintain the struggle to make South Africa the freest on earth. There were times when I thought it was no more than a dream that maybe only my children or their children's children could inherit. After all, such freedom has been the dream of Africans for generations upon generations.

First we prayed to break the yoke of the colonialists, and then we prayed to free ourselves from their successors. After all, each generation learns its values from the preceding generation. We had known only bondage and oppression. We had known only silence and despair. What could be hoped for was something better.

Yet, I dared to dream, as did many millions, so that today we are here in a new South Africa: not always free from the terrors of its oppressive past, but now struggling with the meanings and measure of freedom, dignity, and hope. Imagine how it felt that day, just a little over a decade ago to see Madiba (Nelson Mandela) and so many others who fought with us in the struggle, walking into the light of a new day as free men and women, ready to take up the struggle for a more just and compassionate society. Just as such dreams are coming true for all of us in post-apartheid South Africa, so they can come true for all who long for a healthier and holier time. Similarly, we must take seriously the dream for the future when our children can raise their children without the fear of AIDS. So much in this dream, though, is difficult. For each one of us is called to relinquish our fears and prejudice from the past: our past as Africans, our past as humans, our past as people of faith.

It was once thought that the acquisition of disease was the result of sin. The sin was either due to the displeasure of the ancestors or a sin against the Creator. The belief that one became ill for some offence against nature, God or family was shared by societies around the world. Even today we find aspects of it when discussing fearsome diseases like AIDS. Then, people who were ill were shunned and scorned. They were separated from family and separated from community.

Regrettably, this kind of thinking still has its proponents today in places where many of us live. Many people's experiences of the work of the Church may not be positive and life giving. The Church has committed the grievous sin of silence in the face of discrimination and fear. When it has spoken out, it has, sadly, often spoken out in judgement upon the sick. This is not new. There are many examples throughout human history which indicate that religion has tended to blame those who suffer from disease. All the more reason, perhaps, for religious people to repent of the sin of stigmatization.

Tragically, for too long, those in authority have condemned – either through silence or words of judgement – those living with and dying from AIDS. Too often blame has been chosen rather than compassion; judgement rather than mercy; scorn rather than salvation.

It has broken my heart, and those of many others, to realize that too many children, whose parents have died from AIDS, have themselves been treated like diseased pariahs. Children have been rejected and ignored. Their childhoods, the time of developing values and learning life skills, have been curtailed or distorted because a parent was infected. There are ghastly reports of children being starved in their home communities and treated as outcasts. This is a sin. But it is more than a sin. For in the shadows of hatred and fear we find the fertile soil for planting seeds of the next harvest of this pandemic.

Each day Africa loses more than 5,000 people from AIDS. Every eight minutes there is a new infection. As you read this section, seven people will become HIV-positive. Many will be children, whose self-esteem and hope for life were snuffed out by condemning communities. We must repent of our stigmatization of others, and firmly intend new responses and new life. And we must do what we intend.

There is a crueller dimension to the sin of stigmatization. Stigma is most often created by shame and fear. But there is also stigma fuelled by ignorance of the facts and denial of the facts. Nothing could be more cruel to those infected than to believe that HIV is not the cause of AIDS. The science and research establishments of both the first and third worlds concur that the HIV virus is the virus that causes AIDS.

While it is, indeed, true that other facts like poverty, poor nutrition and other diseases contribute to a compromise of the immune system, and that indeed, elimination of poverty, better nutrition and eradication of disease would vastly enhance, both the length and quality of life, it is still a fact that HIV causes AIDS.

There are still those who sincerely believe that the admission of being HIV-positive is to admit that Africans are uniquely diseased; more so than the rest of the human race. The opposite side of this coin is to hold the belief that somehow Africans are uniquely immune from AIDS. Bitter experience tells us that this is not the case. These mistaken beliefs are sickening and tragic for they make mockery of science and learning. They play strangely into the myth that Africans are less able than the rest of the world.

In reality, there are more reported cases of AIDS in Africa than anywhere on earth. And there are more people living with AIDS in Africa than anywhere on earth. Many of our people were not informed about how to protect themselves and their loved ones soon enough to save themselves and others. Thus the virus spreads. HIV is a virus, not a sin, although in the minds of some they are the same. By hiding from the fact that HIV is sexually transmitted, we tend to make the virus sinful. By loading up on issues of morality we confuse our people in the reluctance to talk about the facts. HIV is transmitted like other sexually transmitted viral diseases. It is transmitted by intimate contact with blood, semen, and some other body secretions. Like other sexually transmitted diseases it can infect the unborn in the womb. By not making these facts clear we separate ourselves from each other as we look for scapegoats to blame. Denial of these facts creates the stigma.

While we have taken the initiative to work toward an end of this pandemic, we Africans have come to realize that our sexual behaviours must change in order to save lives. We have come to see that, while our sexual expressions of love can affirm life, indiscriminate and irresponsible behaviour compromises life. We must be responsible for our behaviour, and we must be respectful to women. We must learn to respect the person who says 'No' to sexual activity, and live by that commitment. And we must teach our young men to respect themselves and respect their partners.

As human beings it is easy to be confused about sex, which is so intimate a part of our lives. Our confusion about sex stems from the fact that sexuality goes beyond mere biological reproduction. Sexuality, in one way or another, pervades our entire personalities. The outpouring of human desire can occur at any moment when sufficient stimulation, biological, spiritual or emotional, is provided. The flood of desire can culminate in sexual and genital activity. How we behave sexually tells us about our acceptance of death.

Obsessive sex can mask the fear of death or at least point to our tenuous grasp on life. When we consider that AIDS, a sexually transmitted disease, is now part of the formula, is it little wonder that denial is so powerful? The sex act which can make us feel that we will live for ever, makes us confront what we fear the most: death. It is both painful and upsetting to think of sex as a means of death. A biological fact has become a shaper of the most intimate expressions of ourselves. I think it is fair to say that our sexual lives in the time of AIDS are challenged in ways that we do not like to think about and could not have imagined.

We must develop new respect for the ancient wisdom of the Church about monogamy as being crucial for our survival. We must acknowledge that the Church's traditional teaching of fidelity is about life, not limitation. We must accept the reality that we have responsibilities to the larger community in our sexual behaviours.

For example, it is clear that we must protect our loved ones and our families by knowing our HIV-antibody status. I fully understand the fearfulness or at least insecurity about this. But to do less than know your status is to commit murder. We must also know the antibody status of our sexual partner, an equally upsetting experience, for these issues strike at the heart of intimacy in uncomfortable ways for which many of us are not prepared. To accept less than knowing our partner's status is to risk our suicide. Suicide and murder are now added to the list of sexual sins.

The Church plays a critical role in shaping the values of a community. It is time to remind the world that compassion is one of our highest values. Our place of value is in forgiveness for those who have made mistakes, those who have had moments of doubt and despair that God can love them. God loves each and every person and God's will for each of us is to have life, and have it more abundantly. There can be hope and help for all. And our message to the world is that Africans are not the cause of HIV and AIDS but, like the rest of the world, Africans are living with and dying from HIV and AIDS.

We are called to have hope for tomorrow. In order to do that, we must deal realistically with today. To stop this pandemic will take hard work. It will take the greatest commitment of governments and their people and faith communities that the world has ever seen. First, we must ensure that everyone who needs medical treatment has access to such treatment. There is a basic human right to health. Second, there are safe and effective pharmaceuticals available today, which can alleviate suffering and extend life. These drugs have proved safe and effective around the world. We know that medical researchers have worked day and night for nearly two decades on trying to find a cure. While indeed there are always risks with every treatment for disease, these risks are acceptable because, in the final analysis, they yield life not death.

We must partner with and empower our governments and people to embrace the commitment for just and compassionate civil societies. As such, we must make sure that treatment is readily available for all who desire it. Without treatment we cannot hope to build a future. Without adequate treatment we cannot prevent transmission of HIV and AIDS from mother to child. We have the tools at hand to prevent the spread of this virus from the first moments of life. Yet in some communities and nations our hands have been tied, either due to ignorance and fear or for economic, social or political reasons.

Scientific research in the arena of diseases of the poor is not nearly as large as it should be (see Jeffrey Sachs' comments on p. 37). This is because there is little profit for the pharmaceutical companies. This is understandable. They are not charity organizations and have a responsibility to their shareholders. I firmly believe, however, that their market share in Africa warrants an interest in social and economic stability – both of which are acutely threatened by our AIDS pandemic. Creativity is desperately needed in order to find a way to bridge the gulf between human needs, scientific research and market forces.

There are no disposable people, there are no losers, there are no have-nots! Each human being is a precious and invaluable child of God. Every human being is a person of inestimable worth. For that reason and that reason alone, we must commit ourselves to saving lives and preventing transmission of HIV.

I have hope and I have the conviction that the faith community can make a difference in the lives of those living with and dying from HIV and AIDS. I am committed to the principle that no one shall die alone, but more importantly no one should care alone. We need each other. We need our communities. We need our families. We need our friends and loved ones. We need all of them to help alleviate the suffering in this, the greatest human tragedy in history. God will give us the strength to do this.

There are no rules on what we should do other than to prevent and control the spread of HIV. To survive and thrive, we must bring our renewed compassion to a world of pain. We are called upon to build more just societies. We are called to extend our care and support to those in need.

I do have a simple vision and a call. It is this. We are working for a generation without AIDS. Before that can come true, we must make AIDS a manageable chronic disease through treatment and control. We must work at extending life through treatment and aggressive prevention. We have the tools to bring this untamed killer into control to the extent that families will not have to be uprooted and communities destroyed.

We can educate our children and help them develop the life skills that will keep them from ever becoming infected. We can rebuild our nations as just and caring societies and we can show the world that Africans can bring life out of death, order out of chaos and hope out of hopelessness. We can secure the future, today. But we must never lose sight of the prize: a generation without AIDS.

In this vision, I see children running freely on our streets; their parents walking beside them. Whole families are together and whole communities are working side by side for better lives for all their inhabitants. This is a vision of Mother Africa and her children at home and at peace. Our traditions of family and community are renewed and give life. Our churches and houses of worship sing again praises to the God who has delivered us into life.

Implicit in this vision as well is the understanding that it will take the rest of our lives and all of our efforts to make it so. God has put us on this earth to make a difference and to be God's heart and hands and feet, where God's people live. We can make the difference.

Facing and working with globalization

An event in one part of the globe has a domino effect on the rest of the world. The buzz word today is globalization, and we need to spell out, albeit very briefly, our understanding of this phenomenon. The way we respond to ethical and moral imperatives posed by globalization will determine to a very large extent the kind of future we fashion for ourselves, our children and our children's children. How we deal with this question will affect the very future of our planet Earth as well as the survival of humanity.

Globalization is market-driven and technology-fuelled. Its main characteristics include a creative dynamism of invention and entrepreneurial risk-taking – which is quite thrilling – and the breaking open of old, honoured traditions when they get in the way.

There are at least five major interconnected, but distinct processes wrapped up inside the concept of globalization. Over the past decade there have been:

- a revolution in information and communications technology;
- massive deregulation in the way in which money is allowed to flow around the world;

- increasingly interdependent and integrated distribution of goods across the world;
- a significant burgeoning of trade;
- continuing growth in the importance of large multinational companies.

While these processes are a reflection of humanity's advancement and are likely to be with us for some time, nevertheless there are three discernible elements of this globalization process which are cause for some concern:

1 The powerful/wealthy are establishing the character, priorities and values of the emerging world order. Their priorities and values are a global free market economic system based on competition, efficiency and productivity. But, all too often, this is at the expense of an increasingly disadvantaged sector. This is creating problems that, in the long term, will threaten world order and economics.

2 A single, lucrative, world market, which is increasingly the site of heated contest, is emerging in the process. Alternatively stated, globalization processes are dramatically extending the reach and depth of the international political-economy as rich developed countries seek world markets for their enterprises. In the process, many poorer countries are being drawn further into the global economic system, but the terms of inclusion are dictated by and favour the wealthy. Others face the spectre of exclusion from economic activity.

3 International markets increasingly favour the economics of scale and collective capacity. That is, competitors with the greatest capacity (those that can instantaneously mobilize vast resources and/or co-ordinate economic strategy across a range of domains) will always be the most effective in competition. Accordingly, prosperous regions are striving for more pervasive political and economic interconnection and integration, and poor regions are increasingly being left behind.

Combined, these three characteristics are resulting in the simultaneous integration but also subordination of poor countries in the international political economy. At the dawn of a new age there are serious questions over whether developing states will be able to survive these globalization processes at all. Poor countries and regions of the world face the danger of permanent marginalization. In economic terms they find themselves consistently 'out-competed' in international markets by the wealthy and powerful.

Global recession and generally depressed international markets for primary export products continue to stifle the export-oriented development drive of most third-world nations. Less developed countries have been forced to accept worsening terms of trade for fear of complete exclusion from international economic activity. For the wealthy, continents such as Africa remain the source of oil and scarce, non-renewable resources. Simply put, in the new age the poor face the danger of designation to perpetual irrelevance.

So, while the powerful plan to become more powerful, the underlying, fundamental result is that the poor countries get poorer, and children are the primary victims. Today we are villagers living in a global village. We have to face these children and take responsibility for what happens to them.

In 1999, according to the Human Development Report of the United Nations Development Programme (UNDP) the assets of the world's top three billionaires were more than the combined gross national product of all the least developed countries and their 600 million people.

This state of affairs poses a threat to the survival of humanity and therefore should not be allowed to continue unabated. Salvadore Marcus says:

> A new world war has begun, but now it is against humanity as a whole, in the name of 'globalization'. This modern war assassinates and forgets . . . As in all world wars what is at stake is a new division of the world. This new division of the world consists of increasing the power of the powerful and the misery of the miserable.

We need to engage now in combating this war by putting in place strategies to create a world with a human face. We need new economic systems which put people, not profits, first.

This effectively means that we have reached the point when a new attitude towards the partnership between the developed and the developing world is needed. For we are dependent on one another. We have to choose life or death. To choose life is the obvious and only option, for it provides a future in all its fullness, not only for us, but also for our children, and for our planet.

With promising developments occurring in many countries, the time is ripe for new partnerships of trust and hope. The world's holistic nature has always been obvious to those who recognize the need for healthy partnerships in which the different cultures of all are respected and understood. Here I would like to quote from the resolutions approved by the Lambeth Conference of Anglican Bishops, 1998:

> Creation is a web of inter-dependent relationships bound together in the Covenant which God, the Holy Trinity, has established with the whole earth and every living being.

1 The divine Spirit is sacramentally present in Creation, which is therefore to be treated with reverence, respect and gratitude.
2 Human beings are both co-partners with the rest of creation and living bridges between heaven and earth, with responsibility to make personal and corporate sacrifices for the Common Good of all creation.
3 The redemptive purpose of God in Jesus Christ extends to the whole of creation.
4 This resolution underscores the need for reverence for all Creation and the upholding of the sanctity of life.

The thrust of globalization: disintegration of community

But true community is also being deeply undermined by globalization. The bonds of traditional community groupings – family, town, nation – are being sheared apart by globalization. Not even national governments are supreme any more. The global market all but dictates commodity rates, exchange rates, interest rates, and capital flows without regard to a people's or a government's preferences. And these massive, lightly-regulated markets coupled with fast and cheap communications make it possible for individuals to gain unprecedented power. Microsoft's Bill Gates, who personifies global technology, has held summit meetings with China's president Jiang Zhemin. And George Soros, who personifies global finance, was popularly identified as instrumental (through his hedge-fund trading) in the collapse of Southeast Asian currency values in 1997. Though one could put a photo of Bill Gates or George Soros on a poster and label it, 'the global man: any nation's equal', each represents the possible extreme. For most people, globalization undermines community in less spectacular, but no less significant, ways. Globalization undermines community by affecting the present, the past, and the future.

The present. With its emphasis on quick response to market demands, globalization deprives the present of stability. One's job may be changed, or eliminated, without warning. I know of an engineer whose assignment was changed six times in the past six months, each time without question or warning. Since globalization is built on technology and information, fewer people are needed to get a job done. Labour just isn't as valuable as it used to be. In this setting, and with ever-changing market demands governing, loyalty between employer and employee is neither given nor rewarded. One middle-manager, frustrated by the callous treatment of people in her organization, decided to talk to the boss to see if human relations could be improved. It would boost morale, she thought. Her overture never developed into a conversation. Instead, the boss laid down a rule: there are to be no personal relations in this organization. There is no time or energy to waste on that.

The sociologist Richard Sennett investigates the flexible, short-term orientation of the global workplace and discovers an attitude in which the work force is considered 'contingent'. Imagine what that means for a worker's sense of stability in the present. Imagine what that does for community in the workplace. The constant threat to workplace survival makes every human relationship equally contingent. If work is short-term then loyalty is impossible. True, globalization sees the widespread use of ad hoc teams to handle projects, and this would seem to promote community. But teams are ephemeral, and they only support a superficial sort of community, devoid of real personal devotion to others and engendering instead a wariness, anticipating the end of the project.

The past. Globalization also degrades community by erasing historical memory. The rate and degree of change is so rapid that the past just vanishes from sight like a dissolving jet trail in the atmosphere. Entire communities lose their memories.

I understand that the city of Livermore in California spent two weeks recently trying to find the time capsule they buried 25 years ago. No one could remember where the capsule was buried, or what interesting artefacts from the town's life in 1974 it contained (although many agreed that there was some good Californian wine in the capsule!). In the year 2000, they buried a new time capsule and this time they decided to mark the burial spot with a plaque, so forgetting would be impossible.

On one level the Livermore story is amusing, but I find in it a sobering lesson. When globalization moves too fast for communities to remember their stories, communities and the individuals within them lose identity, lose self-understanding, lose a sense of being located in a comprehensible sequence of events. Twenty-five years ago what did Livermoreans consider to be special enough about their community to save for the next generation to see? We'll never know . . .

The future. The pace of globalization renders the future unfathomable, bringing change too rapidly to be understood. It's like riding a bullet train: the scenery passes by too quickly. The present becomes the past, the future becomes the present, all in a blur. Of course, for many people the speed of globalization calls up a tremendous energy and unleashes a pulse-quickening excitement, anticipating the possibilities which lie ahead. But many, many other people look to a globalized future with destructive anxiety.

The journalist Thomas Friedman, in his book about globalization, *The Lexus and the Olive Tree*, tells a story about his visit last year to the mayor of a Brazilian town in the Atlantic Rain Forest. Men in this town, for as long as anyone could remember, had earned a living by logging. But the mayor knew that the forest would not last, and he was attempting to attract eco-tourism to his town as an economic alternative. At the end of Friedman's interview, typed out on the reporter's laptop, the mayor had a question: Friedman recalls:

> He looked me in the eye and said, 'Do we have any future?'
>
> His question hit me like a fist in the stomach. It almost brought tears to my eyes, looking across the table at this proud, sturdy man, a mayor no less, asking me if he and his villagers had any future. I knew exactly what he was asking in his question: 'My villagers can't live off the forest any more and we're not equipped to live off computers. My father and grandfather made a living off logs and my grandchildren might make a living off the Internet. But what are all the rest of us in between supposed to do?' I cobbled together an answer . . . The mayor listened, nodded his head, thanked me very politely and then got up to go to his car. As he was leaving, I pulled the interpreter aside and asked him if he could ask the mayor, when they got to the mayor's car, what he thought of my answer. A few minutes later, the interpreter returned. He reported back that the mayor just wanted to remind me of something he had alluded to in our interview: 'When he gets to the office every morning he has two hundred people waiting for him, asking for jobs, housing and food – not to mention out-of-work loggers threatening his life. If he can't provide them with jobs, housing and food, they will eat the rain forest – whether that is sustainable or not.'
>
> (Friedman, 2000)

'Do we have any future?' 'They will eat the rain forest, whether that is sustainable or not.' When the future changes too fast, when globalization makes the future incomprehensible or untenable, a community is pushed out of a constructive, fruitful life together, and into destructive desperation.

Globalization unsettles present, past and future; and all tends to degrade true community. Besides this, the forces and systems which unglue community are hard to get at: they are invisible, impersonal and too big to comprehend. With community seriously depleted, life in the new global environment is typified by the individual, swimming in the fast and treacherous currents of an impersonal, incomprehensible system.

With the degradation of community has come also a moral hollowing-out. Along with the disorientation and self-confusion just described has come a confusion of moral sense. Daily activities and decision-making have become largely unburdened by moral reflection. Instead, successful response to market demand has become the measure of what is good.

Current language reflects the brutality of the global environment: ' "Cannibalization" is the management-speak buzzword of the "new" economy,' reported *The Economist*. 'Nowadays, firms that are willing to undercut their existing business through innovation are seen as visionary. After all, better to cannibalize yourself than to allow rivals to tuck into your market-share.'

And the free-wheeling impersonality of globalization now enables crime and corruption to reach farther and deeper than ever before. As William Greider puts it, 'Big money hides itself in the global economy. Respectable capital mingles alongside dirty money from illegal enterprise (drugs, gambling, illicit arms sales) because the offshore banking centres allow both to hide from the same things: national taxation and the surveillance of government regulators' (Greider, 1998).

At least, along with the good and exciting new horizons and advances of globalization, the negative consequences are visible as well. And right now, some of the most important work the people of the world can do is to search for a global ethic: an ethic which can work universally around the globe. The enormous challenges we face, such as guiding the future of planet Earth and assuring the very survival of humanity, demand that we forge partnerships of trust and hope – in other words, work to reverse the effects of globalization which weaken community. In so doing, it has become urgent that we seek to discover a global ethic which will constitute the basis of our co-operation.

Natural moral law and globalization

The first work of ethics is to define 'the good', and perhaps the most obvious place to start in developing a global understanding of the good is with natural moral law. Embedded in human nature and in the entire natural order is a certain, fundamental preference for the good, although different moral philosophers define this in somewhat varying ways. Every human being possesses a capacity to recognize the good, a capacity which natural law ascribes to God, no matter how one understands God. Even humanists are usually willing to confirm the good of natural law, ascribing the source not to God but to an 'innate goodness' of human character.

Classically, though, natural law does uphold the notion of God, and identifies God as the source and adjudicator of all good. Among these may be counted such foundational good as:

- the sanctity of life;
- the dignity of each human person;
- the responsibility to demonstrate respect and care for the other person;
- the commensurate expectation of being treated with respect and care by the other.

These latter two make up the so-called 'golden rule'.

Sophocles: natural law more authoritative than the state

As long ago as the fifth century BC, Sophocles expressed the concept of natural law in his play, *Antigone*. In this play, Creon, the king of Thebes, had pronounced an edict forbidding the burial of traitors who die on the battlefield. According to the edict, these fallen are to be left where they lie, to be eaten by dogs and vultures. One such traitor was Polynices. His sister, Antigone, revolted against the whole idea and proceeded to bury Polynices. She was of course arrested and brought before Creon. The following dialogue ensued:

Creon: Now, tell me thou – not in many words, but briefly – knewest thou that an edict had forbidden this?

Antigone: I knew it. Could I help it? It was public.

Creon: And thou didst indeed dare to transgress that law?

Antigone: Yes, for it was not Zeus that had published me that edict; not such are the laws set among men by the Justice who dwells with the gods. Nor deemed I that thy decrees were of such force, that a mortal could override the unwritten and unfailing statutes of heaven. For their life is not of today or yesterday, but from all time, and no man knows when they were first put forth.

            (*Antigone*, 450–7, trans. Oates and O'Neill, 1938, p. 28)

Antigone's claim is that the 'imperative of morality', whose basis is 'the unwritten and unfailing statutes of heaven', lays down some obligations with regard to the treatment of human beings. In this particular case, the obligation is that human beings are entitled to a decent burial, irrespective of who they are – whether they are traitors or not. The significance of this story is that Antigone establishes a very important principle: there is a higher law, which is above the law of a state and which holds a greater authority.

Inspired by the Stoic philosophy, Cicero gave the following definition of natural law:

> True law is right reason in agreement with Nature; it is of universal applica-
> tion, unchanging and everlasting; it summons to duty by its commands,
> and averts from wrong-doing by its prohibitions. And it does not lay its
> commands or prohibitions upon good men in vain, though neither have
> any effect upon the wicked. It is a sin to try to alter this law, nor is it allow-
> able to attempt to repeal any part of it, and it is impossible to abolish it
> entirely. We cannot be freed from its obligations by Senate or People, and
> we need not look outside ourselves for an expounder or interpreter of it.
> And there will be no different laws at Rome and at Athens, or different laws
> now and in the future, but one eternal and unchangeable law will be valid
> for all nations and for all times, and there will be one master and one ruler,
> that is God over us all, for He is the author of this law, its promulgator, and
> its enforcing judge.
>
> (*De Republica*, III, 22–3)

Cicero mentions some very significant elements of this law. He states that natural law derives its authority from God. God is its 'Author . . . its promul-gator and it enforcing judge.' He speaks of the universal nature of this law. It is universally applicable to everyone in 'Rome' and 'Athens' alike. He says that its obligations are binding on all people. 'We cannot be freed from its obliga-tions by Senate or People.' Cicero clearly understands humanity as a universal community that is bound together by an eternal order. It is this eternal order that regulates the affairs of people.

St Paul: God the source of natural law, and natural law as ontological

In the Christian tradition, one of the earliest New Testament writers to con-sider the concept of natural law is St Paul. His exposition on the subject of natural law is given expression especially in the first two chapters of the Epistle to the Romans, which displays, among other things, a panorama of the moral failure of the human race – despite the testimony of natural law to guide them. In these chapters, one of the things Paul is eager to show is that there exists a moral order which is common to all people. This order has been revealed by God in creation. In Paul's view, the notions of good and evil belong to the order of nature. Evidence that there has been a general revela-tion of the good is, according to Paul, based on the fact that the Gentiles, who have no knowledge of revealed moral law, nevertheless 'do instinctively what the law requires' (Romans 2.14). Hence, he is able to indict all people for the bankruptcy of their moral behaviour. 'Therefore you have no excuse, whoever you are,' Paul asserts (Romans 2.1). All people, according to Paul – irrespective of whether they are Christians, or Jews, or Gentiles – are under the judgement of God for their failure to perform the good. Judgement is not according to a person's status, but falls on all who 'obey not the truth, but wickedness'. However, there will be 'glory and honour and peace for every-one who does good . . . For God shows no partiality' (Romans 2.8–11).

Thus, we can see that Paul makes two very important points concerning natural law.

1 The good finds its source and definition in God.
2 Natural law is not arbitrary, but conforms to the created order and to created human nature itself.

Thus, God has so created the world so that there are certain universal moral truths which are absolutely necessary for human living.

Thomas Aquinas: ontology of natural law elaborated

This ontological approach receives further elaboration by the Renaissance theologian, Thomas Aquinas, who wrote:

> Supposing the world to be governed by divine Providence . . . it is clear that the whole community of the universe is governed by the divine reason. This rational guidance of created things on the part of God . . . we can call the Eternal Law . . . [Now] since all things which are subject to divine Providence are measured and regulated by the Eternal Law . . . it is clear that all things participate to some degree in the Eternal Law . . . But, of all others, rational creatures are subject to divine Providence in a very special way; being themselves made participators in Providence itself, in that they control their own actions and the actions of others. So they have a certain share in the divine reason itself, deriving therefrom a natural inclination to such actions and ends as are fitting. *This participation in the Eternal Law by rational creatures is called Natural Law . . .*
>
> (*Summa Theologiae*, II/I, 91, 2)

In Aquinas' view, the eternal law is the plan of divine wisdom directing all things to the attainment of their proper ends. 'Hence the Eternal Law is nothing else than the plan of the divine wisdom considered as directing all the acts and motions of creatures.' Aquinas shows quite convincingly that human morality derives from God.

Macquarrie: ontological aspect of natural law contains absolute moral imperative

This ontological approach, undoubtedly, provides a solid ground for the global ethic we are seeking. As the moral theologian John Macquarrie points out, 'To recognize that morality has this ontological foundation is already to perceive it in a new depth. Without such a depth, it is hard to see how there could ever be an unconditioned obligation to which one simply could not say "No" without abandoning one's authentic personhood. There could be only relative obligations, imposed by the conventions of a particular society' (Macquarrie, 1980).

Natural law applied: human rights

An elaboration of natural law, already in operation with a global reach, is represented by the various codes of human rights, including those contained in the Charter of the United Nations. Recent trials, at the Court of International Law in The Hague, of persons indicted for crimes against humanity, put a global ethic of human rights into practice.

According to Professor David Little:

As the notion 'human rights' has come to be understood in contemporary international usage, it means a set of justifiable or legitimate claims with at least six features:

1 They impose duties of performance or forbearance upon all appropriately situated human beings, including governments.
2 They are possessed equally by all human beings regardless of laws, customs, or agreements.
3 They are of basic importance to human life.
4 They are properly sanctionable and enforceable upon default by legal means.
5 They have special presumptive weight in constraining human action; and they include a certain number that are considered inalienable, indefeasible, and unforfeitable.

Natural law distorted by globalization

As apt a foundation for a global ethic as natural law may be, it suffers from having been distorted – curiously enough – by the expansion of globalization. With a long eye backward into history, one can date the beginning of the current era of globalization to the late eighteenth century, corresponding to the later stages of the Age of Enlightenment and matching the dawn of the Industrial Revolution. This era saw the concentration of capital and extension of commercial reach around the globe, with key innovations coming in the transportation sector.

The deist version of natural law

The boom in global economic activity was supported philosophically by deist philosophers, including Benjamin Franklin, Adam Smith, Thomas Jefferson – the framer of the US Declaration of Independence – and Thomas Paine, who wrote *The Age of Reason*. Deism was a form of natural law, as Paine described it:

> The Almighty Lecturer, by displaying the principles of science in the structure of the universe, has invited man to study and to imitation. It is as if He had said to the inhabitants of this globe that we call ours, 'I have made an earth for man to dwell upon, and I have rendered the starry heavens visible, to teach him science and the arts. He can now provide for his own comfort, *and learn from my munificence to all, to be kind to each other.*'

What we discover in the deist brand of natural law is:

- an uninvolved God, expressed in the mechanistic systems of nature which God set up at Creation;
- a reliance on rationalism which favours the power of the human intellect (what Paine calls 'the choicest gift of God to man, the gift of reason'), to the neglect and denigration of non-rational human capacities, and which expects rational humanity on its own to achieve progress upon progress, moving towards utopia (the Tower of Babel syndrome);
- celebration of the individual, with rights protected even at the expense of community, and with ever-narrowing responsibilities towards others (for example, as promulgated in the American Declaration of Independence, and the Bill of Rights contained in the US Constitution).

Counterfeit 'good'

A deist ethic supports certain types of good which, although in keeping with globalization, are inauthentic. For example, the systems of globalization which appear to run on their own and which produce great riches and advances for some, but which also deliver more entrenched poverty for non-participants, obtain their credibility from embedded deist attitudes. The deist implicitly believes that these systems were set up by the Creator, and understands that this is the way the world is supposed to work – according to natural law.

Similarly, for the deist, an individual pursuing his own interests on the strength of rational thought and decision-making personifies human good. Negative consequences for personal relationships, for the social concerns of community, are not particularly important in this light. Everyone may have rights to life, liberty, and the pursuit of happiness – but if any fail to make the best, the rational use of those rights, it's no one else's fault.

Recovering a right understanding of 'good'

Clearly, something is missing from the deist global ethic. And the fact that something is missing stirs a yearning in people. As Augustine of Hippo so truly observed, 'Thou [O Lord] madest us for thyself and our heart is restless until it rest in thee.' So, I believe that the world is yearning for what natural law lacks, an omission which the deist version of natural law threw so starkly into relief. I believe that there is a real place, in developing a global ethic, for Christians to bear witness to the law which is revealed by God in Jesus Christ.

Paul in Athens

St Paul did this brilliantly in an earlier age, during his visit to Athens, the seat of classical moral philosophy. Striking a chord with the news-hungry world in our own day, it appears that the people Paul encountered there were infatuated by the attractions of change. According to the author of the Book of Acts, 'All the Athenians and the foreigners living there would spend their time in nothing but telling or hearing something new' (Acts 17.21). What Paul did was appeal to the appetite for news, and respond to the people's yearning for God, symbolized by an altar of worship which the Athenians did not know how to name. So, Paul named the unknown God: 'What ... you worship as unknown, this I proclaim to you. The God who made the world and everything in it, he who is Lord of heaven and earth ... himself gives to all mortals life and breath and all things ... and he allotted the times of their existence and the boundaries of the places where they would live, so that they would search for God and perhaps grope for him and find him – though indeed he is not far from each one of us' (Acts 17.23–27).

While the rest of the world may not know God, we do. As the Christian contribution to the search for a global ethic, we can name the Unknown God, thus filling in the missing parts of natural law. Here's what we can name, thanks to the law revealed by God in Jesus Christ:

1 Instead of an uninvolved creator God, our God continuously creates and is also deeply involved in creation as Redeemer and Sanctifier: indeed God is known as Love, not in the least uninvolved.

2 Instead of emphasizing rationality at the expense of other aspects of

human nature, revelation shows that human beings have been made by God as body/mind/soul persons.

3 We know that God allows free-will, which human beings unavoidably use against God and against each other. This shatters the illusion that human achievement alone can produce a better and better world: thus, human actions towards the good are only possible by God's grace.

4 God himself exists as persons in community, eternally and inherently in mutual and dynamic relationship: thus, God the Three-in-One, who has made human beings in his own image, has made us to find our identity in community.

Naming the Unknown God then points to a common good which is based, most accessibly, on classical natural law – with deist distortions peeled away and enriched by Christian witness. With this as the basis for a global ethic, these might be included on the list of what is good:

- the sanctity and the quality of life;
- the dignity of each human person – respecting body, mind and soul;
- the golden rule – taken far enough to nourish community life;
- responsible stewardship of the gifts of creation – not necessarily for the most lucrative use, but also honouring the community, recognizing other values besides immediate economic benefit, and considering the interests of future generations.

Seeking the common good

This brief list suggests some of the most obvious 'goods' which might find their place in a global ethic. But 'global ethic' is really only a grand way of saying 'common good'. And there is only one way I know to discover what the common good is: that is, to come together and search for it. How will we do this? Jacques Maritain says that:

> The aim of society is its own Common Good, the good of the social body. The common good of society is their communion in the good life, which is common both to the whole (the society) and to the parts (to the individual).

Maritain goes on to define three essential characteristics of the Common Good:

1 The first is that the common good implies a redistribution among the persons, but it must aid their development.
2 Second, the common good is the foundation of all authority, as it requires that certain individuals be charged with leading the community.

This authority applies to a free people, as opposed to the dominion by a master over human beings for the particular good of the master himself.

3 Third, the common good has an intrinsic morality, which is essentially integrity of life; the good and righteous human life of the multitude. Justice and moral righteousness are thus essential to the common good.

(Maritain, 1971)

Seeking the common good will be an exercise in rebuilding community. So we will need to breach bounds of distance, cross lines of power, discard presumptions of expertise. Seeking the common good will be an exercise in recovering the memory and identity which help us understand who we are, whose we are, and what is good: so we will need to retell our history and recount our stories. And since this takes place in the midst of globalization, seeking the common good will undoubtedly involve e-mail! What will be the result? Who can say what specific global ethic will emerge? But, in the meantime, we can probably define the common good as ... seeking the good, together, in common.

Ethical and moral resources for response

The world's major religions, which influence our moral behaviour, constantly remind us of the dignity and intrinsic worth of each individual human being. There is a recognition that human beings are made in God's image. There is a rabbinic saying that before every human being there walks an angel proclaiming 'Make way, make way for the image of God'. This unique feature of our humanity implies that we ought not to treat fellow human beings arbitrarily and in an exploitative manner. What it does affirm is that human beings hold the future in their hands and that they should act with an enormous degree of ethical and moral standards based on mutual care and respect for one another and for the whole created order.

The world's major religions also understand that God is not just creator but the author of all life. He provided the resources of the earth for the well-being of the created order and continues to do so. From this it follows that our Creator is an hospitable deity. He requires that we too should be hospitable, showing love and tolerance towards one another. This entails, *inter alia*, equitable sharing of resources that God has provided for our well-being as well as participating as equal partners in decision-making processes in the world.

It follows from this, therefore, that in the ordering of the affairs of the world, human values should take precedence over money values. People must be factored into the profit-incentive process. Two years ago His

Holiness Pope John Paul II said: 'The law of profit alone cannot be applied to that which is essential for the fight against hunger, disease and poverty.'

The Holy Father is right. The law of profit alone – it has already been proved – cannot put food in the bellies of the millions – mothers, fathers, children, grandparents, workers – the millions who hunger and starve on the African continent, in Latin America and in Asia – for it is in the developing world where the most people suffer. The law of profit alone will not allow them the drugs they need to treat the most stressful and appalling diseases known to humanity: HIV and AIDS, malaria, hepatitis, tuberculosis. The law of profit alone will not help the majority in the world to climb out of the deep well of poverty into which they have been plunged by a ruthless economic system whose main driving force is greed.

A guiding principle in designing an economic policy that has as its major focus the well-being of humanity is the notion of the common good. In so doing we would ensure that communities and individuals benefited.

To sustain the world we need a new brand of science and technology, and this needs to be governed by a new brand of economics and politics, with a sound moral foundation. Ethics should precede politics, economics and the law because political action is concerned with values and choices. Ethics must, therefore, inform and inspire political leadership to fulfil our obligations as human beings for the well-being of others and our earth.

One only has to watch the stock and bond trading activities throughout the world to realize that in the buying and selling of stocks, little or no thought is being given to the people's lives that may be decimated by job losses as a result. The fundamental human element is missing in these transactions.

The time has now come for action. The inequalities of the world are increasing at an alarming rate. The rich are getting far too rich and the poor are becoming desperately poorer. God looks down and does not like what he sees happening on earth. The Jewish Old Testament prophets called long ago for justice and righteousness in our dealings with one another and our care of God's created order.

When the people of Israel were on their journey to the promised land, God provided a miracle. It was called manna: food from God for all the people to meet their needs for the day. The instruction from God was not to attempt to hoard, but to learn to trust. Some tried to hoard the manna from God and overnight it began to rot and stink. There is a lot of hoarding going on by some and it is beginning to stink! We must stand up and demand action now. If the rich and the powerful do not take action, they, with the rest of the world, will suffer.

The rich nations, and the multinational corporations, must recognize that they cannot continue on the present course of economic growth and exploitation which disregards the consequences upon fellow human beings and the natural world. The rich must recognize that the purpose of life is not just the acquisition of wealth but the development of the world for the good of its inhabitants and the world itself for future generations. This change of attitude has enormous repercussions. We must grasp the responsibilities given to us to care for the future of our people and of our world.

Imagine a world which has a different economic system from that which exists today: a world where profit is not made by focusing only on monetary reward, disregarding any possible negative effects on jobs and lives; but rather, a world in which the powerful multinationals are economically rewarded by a system which values helping others as much as it values profit – balanced and equitable global economic system, where the focus has shifted to meaningful improvement of the lives of the greatest number of people possible. It takes a small fundamental alteration in our thinking to start a movement which could result in quality of life, not just for a favoured few, but for all.

Klaus Nurnberger wrote:

> We are not the only ones who have a right to live on this singular planet. There are contemporaries in grinding poverty. There are future generations who must be given a chance to enjoy what we are enjoying now. There are nonhuman species, which are pushed into oblivion by our mindlessness and greed. In the long run our own worth will be determined by the degree to which *we are capable of recognising and defending the dignity of all the creatures of God, present and future.*

(Nurnberger 1999)

Summary

The Judaeo-Christian injunction, based on Leviticus 25, states that periodically, every seventh sabbath year, we should review our social, political and property arrangements. Every 50 years, the Jubilee year, we should right the wrongs that have been woven over the period into just and equitable economic relationships, relationships between developed and developing countries.

This belief inspired the movement Jubilee 2000 to work internationally to bring about a new world order, whose main characteristics would be good governance, equity and the general well-being of everyone. This began with the campaign for the relief of unpayable debts.

In the contemporary world, economics influences not only the state of the world economy, interest rates, balance of trade between nations and other important fiscal questions, but also the economic outlook for ordinary men and women. It is important therefore to ensure that a caring ethic is practised in economic relations between people and their governments and between international agencies and the people of this global village of which we are part.

Let us seize the opportunity and utilize the resources and technology that are at our disposal for the general well-being of humanity. In this way we will not only be able to eradicate abject poverty in the world, but we would also create conditions for sustainable growth and development, thereby bringing about peace, stability and a good life for all people.

As we tackle this massive agenda, we may hold before us the words of the biblical book of Revelation 21.3–5:

'Look, here God lives among human beings. He will make his home among them; they will be his people, and he will be their God, God-with-them. He will wipe away all tears from their eyes; there will be no more death, and no more mourning or sadness or pain. The world of the past has gone.

Then the One sitting on the throne spoke. 'Look, I am making the whole of creation new.'

Our responsibility – yours and mine – is to spearhead a new world in which this Revelation vision is fulfilled: a world in which the tears of poverty will be wiped away. In South Africa, we have a uniquely African concept called *ubuntu*. Its main philosophy is captured in the phrase 'I am because we belong together' – in other words: I am only a person through other people.

The African academic Professor C. L. S. Nyembezi has described the values of *ubuntu* thus:

- to live and care for others
- to act kindly towards others
- to be hospitable
- to be just and fair
- to be compassionate
- to assist those in distress
- to be trustworthy and honest
- to have good morals.

My hope is that these values will grow and govern the way we deal with each other as individuals and as nations. We must join hands across economic barriers and together step forward to assure not only our economic, but our spiritual future and that of all our children, for ever.

THREE

The Church: the challenges

God has invited all creation to discover its unity and wholeness in God, despite or perhaps because of our brokenness, the many wounds of division arising from our history of colonialism, apartheid, war, violence and the destruction of our environment. This theme permeates every aspect of our life as Christians, from our Bible studies to our worship; from the resolutions of our synod to our pilgrimage of faith as we seek to respond to God's mission in the world.

We have not lived well with our diversity and differences. We have allowed them to form the basis for exclusion, prejudice and intolerance. Ethnic and racial intolerance leading to war, even genocide and the structural evil of apartheid, are telling examples in the last century of our inability to live with inherent differences. Further examples are sexism and the intolerant attitudes of male superiority often violently expressed in acts such as rape. We have created chasms between rich and poor, a product of human greed and lack of caring. Dominant peoples have ignored the plight of indigenous people almost to the point of their extinction. Able-bodied people cease to care about those who struggle with physical handicaps. God's communal nature, as Trinity, confronts us very urgently with God's passionate commitment to enable us to be in relationship with God, ourselves, each other and creation.

Our unique differences need not constitute the basis for opposition but instead suggest the basis for reflecting the diversity which already exists within God and therefore with all that God creates. We would do well to examine critically the ideological assumptions which dictate that unity is founded on sameness.

God created difference. Not only in the making of millions of galaxies and in the immeasurable biodiversity of the universe, but also in the wonderful diversity of the human race. Why did God make differences? I do not know other than to guess that difference in creation teaches us something of the difference within God and invites us to mirror both the divine difference and its unity.

Difference is only one side of the divine/human story. The counterpoint to difference is our mutual interdependence. We are different, yes. But we cannot function, let alone thrive and find wholeness, without recognizing that difference is difference-in-mutual-interdependence. This means that we understand that nothing can stand alone – not the tiniest butterfly or the most powerful world leader is free from interconnection with the giant web of creation.

We long for wholeness in all areas of life. We long for the wholeness of the entire human race. We long for a healed and whole humanity to live and thrive in an environment which is whole, healed of its human-inflicted wounds; an environment of air that is pure, of plants that bloom, of rivers that are clear, uncontaminated, alive and wholesome. We long too for the body of Christ to become whole. A healed and whole body is one in which every limb functions according to its gifts and calling, together in perfect harmony to the glory of its head Jesus Christ. We long for communities of wholeness where there is no violence, no crime, no fear, but rather groups of people who live in relationship with one another recognizing our mutual interdependence and need of one another. Lastly, each of us longs to be a whole person, an individual who, within the love of God, is truly becoming who she or he should be and become as created in the divine image.

The search for and practice of an ethic of relationship in difference must be pursued if we are to gain that elusive full humanity we long for. Living respectfully, lovingly and creatively across our differences is foundational to our work, our life, our Christian community and implies tolerance, forbearance, kindness, generosity, love and justice.

SOME SIGNIFICANT MILESTONES IN OUR HISTORY

About 150 years ago Robert Gray together with his wife Sophie arrived at Cape Town to begin his ministry as the first Bishop of Cape Town. He established centres of Anglican worship and developed an Anglican spirituality that is rooted in the daily reading of scripture and prayer. His three-pronged focus: preach the gospel, build churches and plant clergy, laid a solid foundation for the Church of the Province of Southern Africa (CPSA, which covers Namibia, Angola, South Africa, Lesotho, Mozambique, Swaziland and the Island of St Helena), with its rich diversity and vibrancy in worship, witness and service.

Education

Robert Gray was also appalled at the nature of local education. So he planned to establish a school in the hope that it would become 'a great engine for the extension of the pure faith of Christ throughout that part of the African continent, by the education of a body of devoted clergy and a pious and intelligent laity'. And this is how Diocesan College for Boys, commonly known as 'Bishops', was conceived. It is encouraging to note that four of our current bishops are Old Boys of this school. Robert Gray's vision spearheaded the Church's concern and involvement in education in Southern Africa.

Apartheid

We look back with thanksgiving to the contributions of Archbishop Geoffrey Clayton, Bishop Ambrose Reeves, Archbishop Trevor Huddleston, Bishop Alpheus Zulu, Archbishop Joost De Blank, Archbishop Philip Russell, Archbishop Desmond Tutu and many others in the Episcopal arena who translated protest into resistance against apartheid in South Africa. The courageous leadership of Archbishop Desmond Tutu during the Standing for the Truth Campaign in the latter part of the 1980s, which saw the collapsing of the granite wall of apartheid, is to be singled out for praise. We thank God for the leadership of Archbishop Robert Selby Taylor especially in the ecumenical movement and that of Archbishop Bill Burnett in the renewal movement. We also praise God for priests like James Calata, Walter Gawe and many other clergy and laity whose profound understanding of the dictates of the gospel compelled them to be preoccupied with issues of sound justice.

Religious communities

Over the years the Church has received many blessings through the grace of God active in the lives of its members, not least with the presence and witness of religious communities since 1874. There are eleven communities active in the Province, and two in formation. In the past they were often recognized for their works of mercy, such as education, nursing, care of the disadvantaged, and for theological education and training. Now the call seems to be towards evangelism, counselling and deepening of the life of prayer and witness and the common life.

If God's call continues to the present day; how will the Church discern vocations, and does it support those who are called in our day?

Ordination of women

Another significant milestone in the past 100 years was a resolution passed by the 27th Session of the Provincial Synod that was held in Swaziland in 1992 that our Province should admit into holy orders those women who are called to serve God in the ordained ministry.

There are now women priests and deacons in most of the dioceses of the CPSA. In ordaining women priests the Church took a large step forward in the journey toward the possibility of wholeness. The priesthood became more representative of all God's people. Women were able to take their rightful place sharing sacramental ministry together with men. The Church's ministry has thus been enriched as women bring different gifts, ideas and styles of ministry.

The welfare of clergy and their families

There have been two commissions in the Province looking at the welfare of clergy. One commission under Bishop Mervyn Castle was concerned specifically with the welfare of clergy, while the other, the Stipend Commission, tabled its report at Provincial Standing Committee in 1997 and its recommendations on the clergy package were accepted. However, it is one thing to accept recommendations at a Provincial Meeting. It is another thing to see that these recommendations are implemented. This is a complex issue because there is on the one hand the economic situation of our region and on the other hand the autonomy of dioceses. However, this is a very serious matter and we need to give our attention to it to see how we can ensure that those who respond to God's call to serve in the full-time ministry are able to do so, free of the guilt of not being able to provide adequately for themselves and their families.

Southern Africa is not one economic unit and the difference in the economies of the various countries is considerable. This is reflected in the difference in stipends between the different countries within our province. It is also true within South Africa that where dioceses are located at the economic growth points of the country they are financially better off and are able to offer better stipends than dioceses situated in the rural areas. The complexity of the Southern African economy as a whole is clearly seen in the diverse scale of stipends within the Province.

While some dioceses have made every effort to increase their stipends to compensate for inflation this has not been possible in all dioceses and the real value of the stipend has declined. In addition, tax on fringe benefits and the cost of education and health facilities have all increased in recent years adding considerable pressure on clergy families as they seek to cope financially. In reality most clergy families are dependent on a spouse's income or support from another source to survive.

Some years ago the Province launched an appeal for a pension fund for the clergy. I am pleased that this fund is now operating in terms of the new Pensions Fund Act with a properly elected Board of Trustees. It is now often quoted as one of the best-managed in the country.

As we have reflected on some significant milestones of our past, with thanksgiving, we now look forward into the future in the assurance that God, who is Emmanuel, will continue to be with us. What are the challenges and opportunities that face us?

CHURCH UNITY

The CPSA has also played a significant role in matters relating to church unity. The CPSA took the initiative at its first Synod in 1870 to open up discussion about union with the DRC (Dutch Reformed Church). This came to nothing, but it was a very early example of taking the first step. The CPSA was not very involved in the work of the forerunner to the Christian Council of South Africa, namely the various missionary conferences, except through the presence of some missionaries. But under Archbishop Joost De Blank there was a new commitment to the Council. This was immeasurably strengthened when Archbishop Robert Selby Taylor was Bishop of Grahamstown, and subsequently he was instrumental in encouraging Archbishop Bill Burnett to take on the General Secretary position at the SACC (South African Council of Churches) in 1967.

Archbishop Robert Selby Taylor was inspired by the Lambeth Conference held in the late sixties to move in this direction. When he was in Pretoria, Grahamstown and Cape Town, he took several initiatives which eventually led to the formation of the Church Unity Commission (CUC) under his chairmanship. It was really his commitment and vision which enabled that whole process to get under way. He was, I know, rather sad that the process did not go faster and reach the goals it had initially set for itself. I was personally impressed by the way in which he led the process and by his own willingness to think in new ways, even though he was in many respects a traditionalist.

Much as the CPSA has played its part in working towards church unity, we have by no means reached full acceptance of our diversity. C. K. Barrett in an essay on the future of church union suggests that the fundamental theological work has still to be done; and that this task should be done by theologians, historians and scholars of different disciplines who recognize that the vital component in church history is not sociology but theology.

I believe that these are wise words. Barrett goes on to quote from Canon Greenslade:

If we find a denomination so far sound in faith that it preaches the Gospel on the basis of the Bible and affirms the Apostles' Creed (and a fortiori the Nicene), if we find that it uses the sacraments of Baptism and Holy Communion and that it solemnly sets apart men and women to be ordained by Christ, through the prayers of the Church there represented, as its ministers, and if we find that this denomination, so far as we can judge, has produced the fruits of the Spirit and shows its power to survive, then we ought to assume that Christ has given it a ministry endowed with His own authority and we ought to acknowledge it to be within the Una Sancta. Between any denominations which acknowledge each other ... to be sister churches, there ought, I believe, to be intercommunion and the possibility of an ordered (but not indiscriminate) interchange of ministers, even though there will be not unimportant differences between them. I am not content to say, there should be intercommunion between them. No, there should be, it is wrong if there is not; there is enough unity of spirit to demand it, and to be injured if refused.

Church Unity Commission

In 1995 our Provincial Synod passed a resolution permitting ordained ministers of the Church Unity Commission (CUC) member churches 'while remaining members of their own churches, to exercise such ministry within the CPSA when duly appointed to do so'.

I think that the CPSA has followed Greenslade's opinion. In allowing CUC ministers to preside at an Anglican Eucharist, I would hope that bishops could determine whether or not such ministers have a view of the Eucharist which would be acceptable to Anglicans. Barrett believes that intercommunion is a necessary step before any kind of organic unity can be achieved. It is here where we express our unity in Christ in spite of differences in understanding. We need a statement on the meaning of the Eucharist which both Anglicans and other CUC churches would be able to accept. This is a concern of the Church Unity Commission, and I hope it will be possible for all the churches involved at least to endorse the section on the Eucharist in the WCC report *Baptism, Eucharist and Ministry* (1982).

World Council of Churches

There are other exciting developments in the area of ecumenism, such as the Faith and Order Commission of the World Council of Churches' statement in *The Nature and Purpose of the Church: A Stage on the Way to a Common Statement*. This statement represents the culmination of work specifically directed towards the study of ecclesiology. Member churches are requested to make responses to this statement which will play an integral role in the evolution of a common understanding on the nature and purpose of the Church.

Anglican/Roman Catholic dialogue

The Anglican–Roman Catholic International Commission (ARCIC) in its statement on authority entitled *The Gift of Authority* makes the claim that Anglicans can find a way of affirming the universal primacy of the bishop of Rome; the reverse claim, also being made, is that Anglican bishops exercise the same kind of magisterial authority as the Catholic college.

The Archbishop of Canterbury's initial welcome for the document, while warm, was guarded. He said 'We are on a journey together and are close enough now to make further progress based on significant theological agreements over the last 30 years.'

This document is true to the method originally introduced and sanctioned by Archbishop Michael Ramsey and Pope Paul VI. And it has practical implications which, if implemented to any degree, would change perceptions on the ground: that Anglican bishops should accompany Catholic bishops on *ad limina* visits to Rome, while in return Catholic bishops should attend Lambeth Conferences. This would be a dramatic, but indeed an effective sign that we mean business when we say that it is our desire to reach full and visible unity to which we are both committed. The Anglican theologian Dr Mary Tanner, in her authorized comment on *The Gift of Authority*, can even say that both churches are 'in the process of change as far as the exercise of authority goes' which is shown, she says, by the fact that 'the Roman Catholic Church is looking to strengthen local and intermediate structures'. What will be crucial will be the response to this document from both Communions. *The Gift of Authority* to my mind is a celebration of careful and prayerful thinking and is itself a wonderful gift to our churches and our other ecumenical partners. It will lead us further along this road to full ecclesiastical communion.

The controversial question of the function of the Universal Primate should not be seen in isolation from the whole range of issues governing our understanding of authority. The statement reflects comprehensively on the manner in which Anglicans and Roman Catholics understand and experience the mediation of authority. The statement says: 'Authority is how the Church teaches, acts and reaches doctrinal decisions in faithfulness to the Gospel ...'

Serious efforts towards making a contribution to the visible unity which we seek as Christians, will strengthen the voice of the Church in Southern Africa in the fulfilment of God's mission.

African Anglican/Lutheran dialogue

There have also been some exciting developments on the African Anglican/ Lutheran dialogue. Four consultations have taken place on this dialogue since 1992. The report of the last meeting that was held in Johannesburg in 1997 spelt out the following:

- the goal;
- elements towards declaration of mutual recognition;
- commitments to further steps towards full communion;
- proposals for immediate joint action.

The Johannesburg Consultation also appointed an interim committee to carry forward the preparatory work. At its meeting in March 1999, it defined its vision as follows:

> The vision which guides our deliberations is that of a United African Church with an African identity in which Anglicans and Lutherans are in full communion and visible unity with one another. We look forward to a unique liturgical unity so that we may worship God as one Church. We hope for a spirit of generosity which will accommodate our cultural and regional differences so that we can celebrate our God-given diversity. We commit ourselves to the proclamation and teaching of the gospel as our primary task. We hope to foster Ecumenical fellowship throughout all levels of our Churches and to be steadfast in the task of evangelism, mission and social activities as imperatives of the Gospel of our Lord and Saviour Jesus Christ.

Once more, as the CPSA, we are challenged to seize the opportunity offered to us by God to make our contribution in both the bilateral and multilateral dialogues in the quest of the unity of God's Church in humble obedience to our Lord's High Priestly Prayer: 'May they be one as you and I are one' (John 17.11, 21).

THE ROAD TO WHOLENESS

Violence against women

One of the most horrifying challenges to our wholeness lies in the endemic violence done to women. Current statistics for South Africa indicate that a woman is raped every 26 seconds. There is at least one survivor of rape in every congregation of the CPSA.

Let it be clearly understood that rape is not a sexual act directed towards women who 'ask for it' by dressing provocatively or by being in the wrong place at the wrong time. It is an act of physical, spiritual and emotional violence. It is a manifestation of unequal power relationships, just like other forms of domination such as militarism, racism, political oppression and patriarchy. We the Church need to recognize our complicity in this crisis. We have endorsed patriarchy, either expressly or implicitly. We have failed to speak out on the issue of violence against women. We have, through our ministry, often instructed women to submit to violent and abusive partners, but we cannot condone this situation any longer.

Rape, domestic violence, the denigration of women's bodies, the denial of women's humanity are enormous challenges facing the church, challenges which, if not addressed, will indicate a gross neglect of our ministry. Over half of the members of the CPSA live in constant danger of rape and abuse. We cannot ignore the cries of women's suffering any longer. Our energies in preaching and teaching, in pastoral practice and our own commitment to exposing and challenging violence against women must be directed to making it clear that such violence is completely unacceptable. At both parish and diocesan level we need to provide support (including healing rituals and liturgies) for survivors of rape and their families. We need to seek ways of contributing towards safe houses for women.

Reparation for victims of apartheid

Throughout the life of the Commission for Truth and Reconciliation that was chaired by Archbishop Desmond Tutu, South Africans have listened to the pain and anguish of victims and survivors of gross human rights violations. Perpetrators who fulfil the legal requirements are being granted amnesty which means that they can not be civilly or criminally prosecuted. It is time for us to turn our attention once more to the material needs of those who have suffered the most. Apart from some limited urgent interim reparations, the needs of those who gave evidence to the Truth and Reconciliation Commission have not yet been met. Our understanding of the gospel leads us to a commitment to reparation and rehabilitation which is a form of restorative justice.

The responsibility for healing the wounds of those who have suffered the most is shared by the whole nation of South Africa. For us as Christians our particular concern is with the poorest of the poor. In particular we believe the priority should be to help the elderly, families who have lost their breadwinners, the disabled, and to provide for the education of children who have lost parents. We also need to give attention to the training of unskilled young people who were engaged in the struggle for liberation. We as Christians, indeed all our faith communities, together with all sectors of civil society, need to act swiftly in partnership with government to instil new hope in those who have suffered most grievously.

Poverty and inequality

It is good that so many organizations are using their energies to combat poverty. In South Africa, a coalition of organizations have signed a Declaration of War on Poverty. The alliance includes the Church, the NGO sector, government, trade unions, the UNDP and significantly, homeless people's organizations representing grassroots communities. The declaration describes poverty and the effects it has on the lives of people, opening with words that are relevant to us all:

> The war on poverty and inequality is South Africa's most important priority and our greatest challenge. Eradicating poverty is essential to consolidate the gains of our new democracy. It is a precondition for social justice, peace and security in our land.

A practical proposal is currently being considered: to deal with the problem of cashlessness: it has been proposed that we have a Basic Income Grant (BIG) for all citizens which would be given to all, but clawed back through taxation from those who do not need it. The aim is to meet basic needs, to stimulate economic development, to promote family and community stability, and to affirm and support the inherent dignity of all people.

HIV and AIDS

In an article published in the *Saturday Argus* on 8 May 1999, entitled 'Natal Birth Rate Slides as AIDS Takes Toll', it is stated that for the first time in documented history, the mortality rate in the province has exceeded the birth rate, as more young mothers succumb to AIDS every day. The 1998 Human Development Report stated that the hardest hit sector was men between the ages of 20 and 40 and women between 15 and 35.

Ms Karen Michaels, a researcher for the Department of Demographics, says that South Africa is experiencing one of the most rapidly progressing HIV and AIDS epidemics in the world, with Kwa-Zulu Natal being the worst affected area. She says that if the trends continued, about five million adults would be HIV positive by 2005. That would result in a steep rise in the adult and infant mortality rate, of which Kwa-Zulu Natal has the highest in the country.

At Provincial and Diocesan Synods, and at meetings of Bishops, discussions have taken place on this subject of HIV and AIDS and resolutions made. Some excellent programmes are taking place in some dioceses. I would like to urge that all of us give serious attention to the HIV and AIDS epidemic.

I am involved as a member of its Advisory Board in a National Adolescent Sexual Health Education Initiative. This initiative operates under the brand name 'Love Life', with support from the Henry J. Kaiser Foundation. Statistics indicate that some six to ten million South Africans could die of AIDS in the next 10 to 15 years. This is certainly one of the greatest catastrophes South Africa has ever confronted. Our initiative is targeted at prevention strategies particularly among the 45 per cent of the South African population still under 20 years of age. Our objective is to influence positively adolescent sexual behaviour, to reduce the risks of HIV infection, teenage pregnancy and sexually transmitted disease. Love Life aims to reduce HIV infection among 15 to 20 year olds by 50 per cent in the next five years.

Its focus is to reduce unsafe sexual behaviour and to promote gender equity among South African adolescents. This initiative builds on existing HIV and sexual health programmes and develops innovative new approaches. The initiative uses popular media – music, television, radio – as the principal means of informing young people about the choices and risks associated with sexual behaviour, including unwanted pregnancy, sexually transmitted diseases and HIV and AIDS. The media aspect of the initiative is reinforced by substantial educational materials produced in an idiom appropriate to adolescent readers and distributed through channels easily accessible to young people. A third element of the initiative involves developing adolescent reproductive health services and outreach programmes including a 24-hour nationally accessible Help Line; approximately 500 peer counselling groups across the country; adolescent-friendly advice and counselling centres, and special adolescent-friendly clinics. In addition, the initiative will focus on making the public health service more accessible to young people and more responsive to their needs.

The initiative will establish an identity based on popular culture and will use young voices and young faces to communicate the message. It will be upbeat, optimistic and fun. The goal is to seek out synergistic opportunities to promote the initiative and to make it part of the popular culture – owned and shaped by young people.

Perhaps above all else the Church has the duty to uphold the Christian teaching on the gift of sexuality as finding its true expression in marriage. I hope that the CPSA's report *The Church and Human Sexuality* will continue to be discussed in parishes.

Children and young people

Young people, children and students at tertiary institutions should be our special care. Here is a constituency of our Church who will be the leadership of tomorrow. Their presence in our parishes often goes unacknowledged and their needs ignored. The resources we offer to equip them for faith and life are woefully inadequate.

All children are born with the same innate potential, hope and dreams. How that potential is developed, how their hope is kept alive and how their dreams are realized depends largely upon the environment the child grows up in. Fifty per cent of a child's intellectual capacity is formed by the age of three years, a further 30 per cent up to the age of seven and the balance of 20 per cent from the age of 7 to 18 years. This tells us that a child's environment is crucial to their development. We as a Church need to ensure that our children are given the best possible start in life, based on the values of the kingdom of God – and most of this is essential prior to starting primary school. We need to focus on basic care in terms of crèche facilities, and pre-school facilities for working mothers where the care-givers are well grounded in the love of the Lord. We need to re-examine our role, as a Church, in the formation of vulnerable, and absorbent young minds to ensure that what they are taking in from their surroundings is based on the foundation of Christ, not the warped influence of unacceptable TV programmes and people in our society who are steeped in violence, crime, pornography, and abuse. It is therefore incumbent upon us to engage in creative programmes that are aimed at nurturing and the formation of minds of children and young people in preparation for responsible adulthood.

I hope our Church remembers and acts on the 1998 Lambeth Resolution on Young People whose preface states:

> This Conference: a) recognises and celebrates the dynamic work of God among young people, and their infinite value in the human family. They are for us in the church, as they were for Jesus, signs of the Kingdom of God among us. Their presence and ministry in the church is essential for the whole family of God to be complete. As adults, we confess with deep humility and sorrow that the adult world has created children of war, children abused by neglect and sexual exploitation, and children who are

victims of aggressive advertising. In joyful obedience to God we reaffirm our apostolic commitment to all young people everywhere.

Route markers on our journey towards wholeness

So much for the challenges which confront us. Our task, having identified those challenges, is to begin to search for route markers on our journey towards wholeness. Some route markers have been implied in the challenges themselves:

- working for ways to eradicate poverty and cancel debt;
- listening to the voices of young people and working with them to create their rightful place in the Church;
- creating a climate of safety for women.

One of the potentially most significant contributions on this road to wholeness is the place of education and training for ministry in our church.

Theological education and training for ministry

In the twenty-first century, we are challenged to place theological education and training as a priority in our Church. The Church needs people who have confidence that the many challenges of this century can be met, and who are able to perceive and respond effectively to the major trends shaping the future. Qualitative growth is a prerequisite if we are to be a dynamic church in the new age.

To this end, we must build firm foundations, on the one hand, for ministry, and dynamic leadership, and on the other, in the life of our church. This demands that we intensify the development of programmes for the formation of clergy and laity and also pay attention to the spiritual and academic life of the clergy through the Continuing Ministerial Education programmes. This must seen to be true not only for candidates for the stipendiary ministry, but even more so for those of non-stipendiary ministry. What this means in practice is that participation in formation programmes must become a prerequisite for admission to any church ministry. It is only a matter of justice to give those who are given special roles in the life of the church theological education and training.

Theological education for both clergy and laity should identify those with special skills and leadership qualities and provide them with further education and training. The Provincial Board of Theological Education and Training for Ministry has the responsibility to meet this demand in the life of our church. However, for this Board to be able to carry out its function effectively, it needs the co-operation of the dioceses by releasing those candidates who have been so identified.

The Continuing Ministerial Education programme has the aim of equipping specifically, but not exclusively, the clergy of our church to fulfil their roles. It seeks to prepare them to take up new and more challenging responsibilities by strengthening their knowledge of key social, theological, pastoral and biblical issues. All clergy should stay abreast of developments in the field in which they are operating. The College of the Transfiguration organizes and facilitates these programmes on behalf of the Provincial Board of Theological Education. They are now held regionally as well.

In my recent ecumenical visit to the Church in Germany, I held extensive discussions, among other things, about possible ecumenical co-operation in the field of theological education and training for ministries. We affirmed the famous Lund Principle: 'Do not do alone what we can do together'.

Embracing our differences, finding wholeness

We stand at the beginning of a new millennium with all the challenges that this presents. As the Church, and here I mean Church in its broadest context, we need to consider very carefully what will be demanded of us in this new millennium. How will we as a Church continue to walk with Christ 'along the way' in a world that is rapidly becoming a global village and where technology will continue to develop at an ever increasing pace? This is a question that requires careful study and deliberation at an ecumenical level. Just as apartheid was too great for one denomination to tackle on its own, so these issues are too great and we need to face them together.

The demands facing us are considerable and I have highlighted just some of them here:

- the healing of the nations;
- the strengthening and empowering of the local church;
- developing an engaged and authentic spirituality.

If we are going to be able to do this work and face the future we need a membership that is deeply committed to the work of God and his Church, and to being agents of his healing love within the context of their lives, at work, at home, and at play. Our faith, our spirituality, must lead us to an ever deepening love for God and his Church that finds its expression in the dedication of our whole life. So often we see this dedication only in terms of the ordained, but as the Second Vatican Council stated:

By reason of their special vocation it belongs to the laity to seek the kingdom of God by engaging in temporal affairs and directing them according to God's will.

We are all, clergy and laity, called to a life of dedication to God and to see the world as the place where we live out this dedication. We must never forget that God, who called Bishop Robert Gray 150 years ago, is the same God who stands before us now and calls us to be his Church as his world continues through this new millennium.

We need to look beyond ourselves to become heralds of God's compassionate presence in the world. Ours is a world where many are experiencing brokenness daily. As God leads us on this journey to wholeness, so he calls us to reach out to others and in the words of Henri Nouwen, to become 'wounded healers', real people on a journey to wholeness, living among, working with, and reaching out in love and compassion to those who are broken in this world.

JOYFUL SERVANTS FOR GOD

A servant with this clause
Makes drudgery divine;
Who sweeps a room, as for thy laws,
Makes that and the action fine.

George Herbert, who wrote these lines from 'Teach me my God and King', had never been a domestic worker. Only someone who has never had to scrub floors, wash windows, clean up after others, day after day, can possibly suggest that drudgery is divine. Similarly, romantic ideas about the spiritual benefits of poverty come only from those who have never been poor. So too romantic ideas about the value of being a servant are propagated by those who are not servants. How easy it is to romanticize being a servant for God; but the image is a painful one for many who are servants. It is also a dangerous image – one used by people in power to keep others in a place of subservience.

Another well-known hymn illustrates this. 'All Things Bright and Beautiful' has a verse (usually now omitted) which runs:

The rich man in his castle
the poor man at his gate
God made them high and lowly
and ordered their estate.

The implication of this kind of thinking is: 'If God has ordained that some should be rich and others poor, who are we to question?'

The servant model

So why today should we even talk about being servants for God, let alone *joyful* servants? How does this imagery come into our Christian lexicon? It is, of course, because Jesus portrays himself as a servant. The Gospel of John tells the story of Jesus who, on the night before his crucifixion, washes the feet of his friends before they sit down to supper together. By this profound action, he expresses the model of true discipleship, which is to perform simple acts of service for others. But this is no ordinary servant and so a word of caution needs to be expressed, lest we adopt the model unthinkingly.

Let us pause a minute and reflect on who Jesus the servant is, what service he offers and what effect that has. Jesus, as portrayed by the writer of John's Gospel, is the divine Christ, the incarnate word of God. It is this incarnation of God, who strips off his outer clothing and washes the feet of his friends – thus taking on the job usually performed by the most menial slave. It is precisely because he does what is *not* required of him that he redefines the meaning of servanthood. He is clearly not glorifying the situation where some people are held in a relationship of subservience to others; in fact quite the reverse. He is challenging this model of relating by offering an entirely new vision of relationships.

He is challenging what one writer calls the 'domination paradigm'. The domination paradigm gives rise to, and sustains, unequal relationships, in which one person is more powerful and therefore regarded as better than another. It works on the basis of non-reciprocity. It is the model with which we are familiar because that is how our institutions in society work. We are accustomed to a few people having power and control over others. We are accustomed to the majority being considered less important. Unity and stability are achieved by the imposition of power and authority.

Jesus seeks to undo this kind of relationship. He does not claim his divinity and then exercise power and control over others. As Paul tells the Philippians, Jesus does not count equality with God as something to be grasped. Instead, he washes feet. He gives away his power and offers a service of love.

It is important to recognize that it is because he has power that he also has the power to give it away. All too often in church and society leaders have defined certain people, especially women, and more especially black women, as servants. Then it is impressed upon them that they should not complain, but be glad to be servants because that's what Jesus was. This is to miss the point entirely. Jesus chose to be a servant because he was free not to be. He chose to be a servant because he wanted to challenge those who claim power and authority over others. What is even more extraordinary about this revolutionary act of Jesus is this: in washing the feet of his friends, Jesus shows us that this is how God relates to us. Jesus shows us that God does not have, nor want, power over us. God wants to serve us, to be our friend, to wash our feet. I know that this is not the picture of God that has been taught to us by the Church. But stop and think for a moment. Who has offered us the picture of God as the powerful ruler? It is of course those who themselves long to be powerful rulers – men, the clergy, those who enjoy having people serve them.

It is not the model of Jesus, though: he does not ask others to serve him. He invites them to be his friends and, on the last night of his life, he feeds them with his own body and blood, his life. If this is how Jesus relates to people, it is how God relates to people – not as ruler, but as servant and friend.

The Christian message is radical, because it challenges all models of power. Those who have power, or aspire to having it, dislike this concept, and so the radical nature of Jesus' example is glossed over and lost.

We see the domination paradigm and its devastating effects on the 'little people' wherever we look in church and society. I became involved in attempts to end the terrible taxi/bus war in the Western Cape, and one day I was privileged and challenged to meet a group of women who live in Khayelitsha. They are ordinary women who struggle hard to earn a living, many of them working as servants of other women. But they struggle not only against poverty. They struggle against domestic violence and disease. They struggle to educate their children. In short they struggle against patriarchy – that evil social system that deems men to be of more value than women; that says men should have power. And they do: it is men who make the decisions to become involved in the war, to perpetuate it, to negotiate around it. All the while, it is women and the children they try to raise and nurture who bear the brunt of these decisions. There are examples of domination all around us.

The role of women in society

What does it mean for women to be called to be joyful servants for God? Should we just abandon the image as being simply bad news for women who are already held in subservience by so many structures in church and society that they really do not need to serve any more? Or can we give this call to servanthood any meaningful interpretation?

First, we can be servants of God. This is not to imply a kind of grovelling subservient relationship with God. As we have seen through Jesus' own example, God invites us to a relationship that is much more whole, healthy and life-giving. God invites us into a relationship of mutuality. God invites us to be God's friends, co-workers, co-carers for creation, co-lovers of the people God loves and sends us to love.

We can be servants of God because God has already served (and continues to serve) us. To be a servant of God means serving the same purposes as God's – what we term the kingdom of God. The kingdom of God is what Jesus proclaimed – justice, peace, care for all creation, recognizing *every* person as being infinitely valued by God and therefore deserving of food, shelter, safety, beauty, dignity and love. Being a servant of God entails remaining faithful to the vision Jesus proclaimed and remaining hopeful and trusting in the face of seemingly hopeless situations.

Second, to be servants of God women need to discover the strength they already have simply because every person is made in the image of God. It is true that the power of women is not the power of political, social or religious rulers. It is a power which Jesus himself endorsed. It is the power of love. It is both inspiring and humbling for me to see women who should long ago have given up in the face of poverty, violence, oppression and hardship, continue to look for ways of bringing life and wholeness for their children.

During the course of the various national poverty hearings I attended, I was struck time and again by the faithful hope of women, especially women in the rural areas, who, against all odds, care for their children, the old and frail, the physically and mentally challenged. They do so on incomes so meagre as to be negligible. They do so despite tremendous physical hardship. Many of these women walk for up to four hours a day simply to collect water.

What keeps these women going? What keeps them serving the young and old and frail? I believe it is hope and love, such as few of us can imagine. What a tremendous power that is; far beyond the power of political or business or church leaders. It is the power of the human spirit, the power of love. As the resurrection shows us, in the end love does outlive hate. May that hope continue to sustain those who hope against hope, who keep loving in the face of hatred and violence.

However, this second suggestion is not to endorse a perpetuation of the status quo. Women should be challenged to see that they have been complicit in surrendering to a man-made world, a man-made God, a man-made church. Women need to become servants and supporters of each other. No longer is it adequate to hand over power to men. Women need to work together for the end of patriarchy.

There is something called internalized oppression. In the context of patriarchy, it refers to the situation where women themselves believe that neither they, nor any other woman, is of as much worth as a man. Women need to free themselves from this form of oppression too, and work together, support each other. This can happen in simple ways, such as ensuring women elect women to serve on church councils or in secular government, or on school boards. It may mean women organizing together to challenge the government's spending on the military rather than health care.

It may mean the simple but effective resistance offered by a community of women in the Pietermaritzburg area. Sick and tired of domestic violence, they devised a scheme to shame those men who abuse their partners. Whenever a neighbour hears a woman being abused and beaten, she goes out on the street with a pot and starts to beat it with a spoon. When other women hear her, they too come out. All stand in the street and beat their pots to indicate in which house the abuse is taking place and to shame the man who is abusing his partner.

We need to recognize too, that not all women suffer the same degree of oppression. Historically, and still today, white women have been oppressed by patriarchy, but they have not been legislated against by apartheid. White women have had access to better schooling, better economic opportunities, better health care, better safety. Women who have power, however limited, need to be encouraged to share it with others, rather than perpetuating the domination paradigm by exercising authority and control over others.

It would be wonderful if the women of our Church could take a lead in helping us to transform our Church. I envisage a transformation from a hierarchical, 'domination paradigm' Church, into a servant Church, where the values of mutuality, courage and faithfulness, rather than power and authority, mould us into the body of Christ.

Having made these suggestions, I perhaps need to add a note of caution. Prescribing what the Church, society or women should do is the patriarchal model. I do not want to perpetuate that. I offer here only some thoughts, some aspects of my dream of a more whole, just and life-giving world. You may have your own dreams. I encourage you to share them because, together, as we unravel what we have called the domination paradigm, we might use those threads, those dreams to weave a rich new tapestry. As we weave together a new fabric of wholeness, humanity, peace and justice we the weavers become what God invites us all to be – joyful servants of God.

AFRICANS AND WOMEN IN SOCIETY

It is perhaps ironic that I, a man, am writing about this subject. However, I am also an African and that, I believe, is significant for two reasons. First, this challenges the narrow parochialism into which it is so easy for all in the Church to fall; and I will say more about this later. Second, being an African is significant because many of the struggles that women face in the

Church and society are similar to the struggles of African people. So I am not wishing to speak for women, but I am speaking from the context of Africa, trusting that some of the insights and experiences of Africa will resonate with the experiences and insights of women in all parts of the world.

What is this context? Africa is a continent of enormous cultural wealth and diversity. It is the poorest continent on earth. Its per capita death from AIDS is higher than anywhere else in the world. It is a continent where in some places, such as Nigeria, the infant mortality rate is 84 in 1000, five times higher than other developing countries (McGreal 1999). Africa is a continent which suffers devastating drought, famine and flood. It is a continent in which major wars have been and are being waged. It is a continent which has been colonized and plundered and continues to be held in colonial captivity by virtue of its economic dependence.

More specifically, though, I am a South African and speak from that context: a context as complex and paradoxical as anywhere in Africa. Mine is a country which is upheld internationally as an example of hope and possibility for many, and yet it is a country plagued by violent crime. In Cape Town, the city where I live, gang warfare is rife. It is a country where our new democracy is celebrated; yet many of its children go to bed hungry at night, have inadequate medical care, little or no access to education and few employment opportunities.

The place of women in South Africa is even more complex.

Our government has one of the highest numbers of women parliamentarians in the world, yet very few women are in positions of leadership in our Church. On the brink of the twenty-first century, women in some parts of the country are still being accused of being witches and are killed as a result of such accusations – a phenomenon not seen in America or Europe for centuries. In our new democracy, with one of the most progressive constitutions in the world, which seeks to protect all persons, we still have a long way to go in making rape unacceptable. While the Americans have had ordained women in ministry since 1974, here, in my own province, the first women were ordained just short of 11 years ago, and there are still dioceses in the CPSA where bishops will not ordain women.

Africa is a continent still racked culturally, economically and socially by the after-effects of colonialism. Decades of economic plundering of natural resources and human labour have left Africa cripplingly indebted to European and American countries, multinationals and organizations. Just as women have been socialized into accepting that menial labour, lower wages and poorer working conditions are their lot, so too, Africans have come to accept that raw materials are drawn from Africa and manufactured elsewhere, that technological skills and higher wages belong to people of the northern hemisphere and not to the people of the southern hemisphere.

Africans learnt well the lessons of the settlers who scorned local culture and tradition and imposed a western Christian culture. One of the heart-felt cries of the Church in Africa today is for Africanization: a rooting of the Christian faith in Africa, using African stories, symbols and models to interpret the faith, and affirming the goodness and wholeness of African culture and tradition. In this, it is not dissimilar from the feminist movement in its aims to critique patriarchy and lend support to the transformation of the Church into a more inclusive, whole and healthy place for women and men. As patriarchy has devalued women, taught them that they are of less worth than men, so too colonialism taught Africans that their traditions and culture were uncivilized and unchristian.

Africans and women have lessons to unlearn together. And it *is* important that we unlearn and learn together. Despite the widely acknowledged global village, in many places the church seems to be retreating into a narrow congregationalism, which denies our membership of a worldwide Church and our interdependence upon one another. One of the great riches of the Anglican Church is its rich diversity. However, both here in the United States and elsewhere, we see individuals and congregations seeking to break away from the larger body for reasons of difference and an unwillingness to live with and wrestle with differences and otherness. We have seen the development of flying bishops in the Church of England, to counter the effect of the ordination of women. Congregations unwilling to grapple with issues of sexuality break away from our broad family. Not only, therefore, because our African and feminist concerns often coincide, but also because we are one Church, I think it is important that we share with one another our insights, concerns, hopes and dreams. What then, are some of the contributions which we in Africa can offer to our search for a more whole, inclusive and Christ-like Church?

Understanding our humanity

It has been correctly said that African people have a sense of the wholeness of life. Religion or spirituality is not a separate department, nor is the religious community separate from a 'wider' community. The life of the community *is* religious, and it has no separate secular dimension. The sacred/secular dualism which feminist theology seeks to challenge simply does not exist in the African world view. However, through a Christian perspective which labelled as syncretistic, 'unchristian' and 'ungodly' traditions and practices of African society a new dualism emerged. Allow me to offer some concrete

101

examples of what I am speaking about. In a number of Southern African communities, it is customary to slaughter a cow and invite the community to a feast to celebrate the birth and naming of a child. However, some missionary Christians proclaimed this a pagan practice, with the result that many families will bring a new-born child to church for baptism, and then, as an entirely separate ceremony, go home to slaughter and feast. Two rituals which, if linked, could provide both a powerful witness to the significance of the new life begun in baptism as well as joining the community in a traditional celebration of new life, become separated. The sacred and secular are separated.

Similar contradictions emerge at the unveiling of a tombstone of a deceased member of the family. Traditional African belief may regard the event as an opportunity to receive the deceased in another mode of existence as a living spirit in the company of ancestors and saints, while the church regards the occasion as one of thanksgiving for the life of the deceased. Again the two sets of beliefs exist alongside one another, but the traditional beliefs are largely unspoken before the Christian minister. However, modern African theologians, along with feminist theologians (and Chung Hyun Kyung here springs immediately to mind) remind us that there is no 'pure' form of Christianity. It all comes in a cultural package. Instead of rejecting or outlawing traditional cultural practices, these should be celebrated, allowing an enriching of faith as well as its rooting and grounding in a particular community. The women's movement has done well to remind us that religion is not separate from domestic life, from childbirth, from friendships and conversation. No part of life is excluded from relationship with God.

There is a saying in many African communities that a person is a person through people: 'We are, therefore I am', the saying goes which underlines our African understanding of humanity. In other words, we discover our humanity in relationship to others. Tiyo Soga (1829–71, the first African minister to be ordained into the Presbyterian Church in South Africa) speaks with and for Africa when he says 'Thina ma Afrika singumzi wobuzalwana nobuhlobo ngokudalwa' ('By nature we Africans are a family of friendship and relatedness'). This insight is not unique to Africa, but it is so profoundly entrenched here, that one cannot begin a discussion on what it means to be human, without this understanding. And it is an understanding which is very different to many traditional Christian anthropologies which concentrate on the individual, the individual's sins, and the individual's salvation. However, in Africa my identity, and indeed my salvation, is not separated from that of the community to which I belong. This understanding of what it means to be human offers an important challenge to the individualism that is prevalent, not only in the west, but in many urban settings in my own

102

country and which is manifested in the church too, in the congregationalism I have just referred to. When we refuse to allow difference in our communities and when we ostracize those who are 'other', we deny ourselves and others the opportunity to be fully human. African culture invites us to embrace the 'other', to recognize ourselves in the 'other' and to discover a fuller and richer humanity. This understanding of our humanity echoes, of course, the profound insights offered by the Christian doctrine of the Trinity, which celebrates a loving communion of free, self-determining, creative persons. Lest it should be thought, however, that women are free, and encouraged to find their fulfilment in African culture, I hasten to add that many African societies are patriarchal. Traditional communities have rigidly defined roles for women and the idea of a woman free from suzerainty of her father or husband is rare. Equally rare is the idea of a woman who has a profession of her own or who chooses not to be married. Here there is much that feminist theology has to offer by way of a different vision for women in African society. I shall say more of this when I come to look at issues of leadership and power. So too, the opportunity for most African women to explore spirituality or even to find space and time for quietness and stillness is a luxury few can afford. Most African women in traditional societies are homemakers, child-rearers and farmers. In the less traditional, more urban environments in South Africa women are frequently the only breadwinners, mostly through domestic work which usually entails travelling long distances daily to the more affluent areas of the city. The cities themselves are violent, the threat of rape and mugging ever-present. Though no longer on the statute books, racism persists, and black women suffer the triple oppression of race, class and gender. Just how far we have to travel in the search for a communion of kenotic, embracing love, which not only accepts but rejoices in diversity, is illustrated by the story of Gugu Dlamini. Gugu Dlamini lived at KwaMancinza, near the east coast city of Durban. She was HIV positive, and chose to tell people in her community of her status so that she could use her position to heighten awareness of HIV and AIDS and help in the fight against the disease. She was killed by members of her own community, a scapegoat for their anger and fear. Her femaleness, her willingness to name her illness, her 'otherness' was too fearful for those who took her life. The dream of community is still a long way off as we in South Africa look for ways to heal the divisions.

Images of God

Notwithstanding the view of some Christian missionaries to Africa that Africans have no concept of God, in the African world-view God is an all-pervading reality. The way African people experience God is portrayed in the names given to God – names which are descriptive of God's character. For our purposes, though, what is interesting is that God is not imaged simply in male terms. Some say God is father. Others say God is mother, or even grandparent. It is indeed only through the introduction of Christianity that many African Christians are willing to abandon altogether traditional cultural and religious ideas and subscribe to a gendered notion of God who gives priority to males above females. African understandings, *despite* being shut out as pagan and uncivilized, have much to offer current theological debates about the masculine notion of God.

The experience of women in Africa, however, does provide the opportunity for a re-evaluation of some of the classical understandings of the Christ. African women's experience is unquestionably an experience of struggle – struggle against poverty, disease, oppression, war. The Christology of African women is thus centred on Jesus the friend, liberator, healer and companion. God in Christ affirms the goodness of women, helps them bear life's burdens and challenges those who oppress women. So that even where the images of traditional African culture have been lost, there is access, through Christ, to God who is love.

Issues of leadership and power in Africa

I referred earlier to the fact that African culture is patriarchal and excluding of women. One of the areas of life where this is most apparent is in the organization of leadership in traditional society. In Southern Africa, the leaders of families, clans and tribes are hereditary leaders and always male. Their power is far reaching, and unchallenged even by healers and prophets. So as much as Jesus' radical egalitarianism and servant leadership is a challenge to church and societal hierarchies in the West, it is perhaps even more so in Africa – a reminder that traditional culture cannot be uncritically assumed to be helpful in indigenizing the Christian faith. However, leadership in African communities, while exercised by men, is always exercised in consultation with the community (including the community of the ancestors), so leadership should not be seen as the equivalent of a totalitarian autocracy.

The whole question of power is probably one of the most important issues to be addressed by the Church worldwide. Christianity, we are aware, was shaped and formulated in the context of the Roman Empire and has in its organizational structures been modelled on imperial hierarchies since the fourth century. Jesus' subversion of traditional power structures (for example by washing feet, and by befriending the undesirables and outcasts) has been systematically ignored by the Church throughout its life. One of the concerns of women is that the ordination of women, far from changing the situation, will simply lead to the creation of female clericalism alongside male clericalism. African women justifiably comment that Christianity, far from liberating them, has simply set up an image of western middle-class woman-hood that has no relevance for Africans. One model of domination has been replaced by another.

Perhaps now is a good time to evaluate the *effect* of women's ordination on the ordained ministry generally. Has the ordination of women changed the shape and style of ministry? Has the Church seen the evolution of a ministry that seeks to serve rather than be served? Has the introduction of women's voices in the north also led to a listening to the women of the south?

The journey of hope for the world

Christianity has ancient roots in Africa. Origen, Tertullian, Cyprian, Augustine of Hippo, to name just four, are African theologians who have shaped Christianity. Africa has contributed significantly to Christian theology in the past, and I am suggesting that it has the potential to do the same today. African Christians, among other liberation theologians, have helped to expose the biases of Western Christian theology which has excluded some and led to the domination of others for centuries. African theology – so named for the first time in 1965 at the All Africa Conference of Churches – is concerned to draw into creative dialogue the Christian faith and traditional African culture. This dialogue, while primarily for the people of Africa, has resulted in fresh insights for Christian theology more broadly, for example in reconsidering the value of non-canonical writings, including local myths and stories. African woman theologians in turn, in 1989, established the Circle of Concerned African Woman Theologians, which has promoted the writing of African women. Mercy Amba Oduyoye is probably the best known of these women. And again, while their writing is specifically for the women and men of Africa, their insights are of immense value for all who espouse liberation, who seek ways to transform the church and society.

In the dialogue between north and south, or Africa and America, Africa, as in the early centuries of the Church, has much to offer Christian theology. If I were asked to identify the single most important aspect of this contribution, I would identify the concept of hope. How ironic that sounds, given some of the statistics I quoted earlier. How can a continent plagued by war, famine, AIDS, poverty, offer models of hope, especially to the north, with its economic prosperity and all that goes with it? I would like to suggest that it is in Africa, in the face of war and famine and disease, that we know our need of God. It is among the women of Africa that we treasure a Christology which reminds us of Jesus' special care for the little ones and the outcast. It is in the face of the struggle to find our identity and express our Christian faith in a uniquely African way that we discover the riches of every tradition and culture. Are not these signs of hope precisely what our rather tired, cynical twenty-first century world needs? Rather than riches and success and self-importance, is not the message of Jesus that those who know their need of God are those who are blessed (Matthew 5.3)?

Professor Lesslie Newbigin, a one-time bishop of the Church of South India, was returning to his homeland, England, after doing missionary work on the Asian subcontinent, and was asked, 'What is the greatest difficulty you face in moving from India to England?' His answer was straightforward and carries with it a strong message. He said, 'The disappearance of hope. Even in the most squalid slums of Madras, there was always the belief that things could be improved. In England, by contrast, it is hard to find any such hope.' This world is a place where we can easily become despairing, yet we dare not be hopeless. The 1978 Bangalore Commission on Faith and Order described hope thus: 'It is a resistance movement against fatalism. Those who believe in God know the power of His love. It is this love that creates persons and societies.'

All of us, from industrial and developing countries alike, should commit ourselves to a hope that refuses to accept an unjust and tarnished world order. My own country, South Africa, has its own special contribution to make in this discovery of hope. What sustained us even in the darkest moments of our history was the unshakeable faith in God who reigns supreme in the world and wills only what is good for the whole of creation. The miracle of a relatively peaceful transition from apartheid to democracy can, to a very large degree, be attributed to the goodness of God. Despite 300 years of colonial, racial oppression, and 50 years of a campaign of terror, we have experienced two peaceful democratic elections and several years of democratic government. We are, against all the odds, learning to be an inclusive society. Yes, Africa, astonishingly, has this message of hope to offer. And just as in the past, an extraordinary ordination offered a sign of hope to members of a despairing Church, so too Africa has this sign to offer today. In some ways they are two very different signs, and yet both suggest that we should, as Christians, always be looking for, namely the hope that out of death comes new life.

One of the major challenges facing the Anglican Communion is to discover ways of strengthening the bonds of affection which bind us together through the inculcation of an ethic of living with difference and otherness. We are different, and our Church is a Church of enormous differences. But our God is also a God of difference and diversity. That is the essence of the Trinity. The mystery of the Trinity is that in their unity, the persons of the Godhead are preserved in their separate relatedness. As human beings, created in God's image, we too are invited to reflect that unity in diversity. We live as distinct individuals, and yet are part of a web of relationships. We need to acknowledge our differences, and respect one another's uniqueness, but these differences need not constitute a basis for opposition. Instead they suggest the basis for reflecting the diversity of God, and all of God's creation.

Is this then the indication of where our journey should now take us? From our different sides of the world, with our different experiences and different expressions of the Christian faith, we have the opportunity to challenge parochialism. We have the opportunity to challenge the cynicism and hopelessness of our world now, and in the future. We have the opportunity to challenge the exclusivism which prefers men above women, whites above blacks, rich above poor, straight above gay. Our Triune God invites us to demonstrate that in our very differences, we can embrace one another, celebrating otherness, and discovering our deep, Godly unity in those differences. God invites us to celebrate the different gifts which women and men bring to the ordained ministry and the diversity of the human family in the Anglican Communion. God invites us to live lovingly across our differences, with tolerance, forbearance, kindness, and generosity. And if this sounds like an impossible dream, God invites us to trust his own transforming power at work in us to bring us to our full potential as human beings who are created in God's image.

For this is a *kairos* moment: we are at the doorstep of the next thousand years in the history of humankind. The first Christians stood on the threshold of the first millennium in a state of hopelessness after the crucifixion of Christ. But God raised him from the dead: hence our age is one of hope, an age of new beginnings, an age of the resurrection faith.

THE ANGLICAN COMMUNION

One of the great joys of recent years in our Anglican Communion – which found considerable expression at the 1998 Lambeth Conference – has been the recovery of narrative (story-based) theology as a means of articulating the gospel. For a renewed recognition of narrative theology is of course one means of our celebrating our diversity as a Communion, when we are invited to attend to the huge range of stories and narrative traditions from across the globe. It is also an important way in which we may learn more of the particularity of our various traditions and achieve an appropriate – and necessary – sense that it is precisely through the particularity of our experiences that God speaks in and through us – that God's Eternal Word is made incarnate – all of which ought to lead to a greater degree of unity and resonance across our global Anglican family.

A narrative that was originally from Ghana, published by Bishop Christopher Gregorowski, helps to narrate more of the unfolding story of our Anglican family.

Fly, Eagle, Fly!

The story begins with a farmer who sets out one morning in search of a lost calf – a calf which the farmer's sons were unable to track down amidst a storm before night fell the previous evening. It continues with the search itself, as the farmer crosses valleys and scales mountains and cliffs in search of this calf which is lost. Yet amidst this search – as the farmer climbs a gully – he finds not the lost calf but an eagle chick newly born and blown – it seems – from its nest during the storm the previous day. So the farmer brings back to his kraal not the lost calf but a newly found, newly born eagle-chick which he gives to his wife and children to place with the other chickens and hens on the farm. And as he gives it to them he says: 'The eagle is the king of the birds, but we shall train it to be a chicken'. Now after a while, as the eagle grows up among the chickens and learns their ways, it of course comes to look more and more distinct, daily to look more and more unlike any previous chicken they have had on the farm. In this it arouses much curiosity until one day a visitor to the kraal questions the farmer about this so-called chicken. 'That's not a chicken,' the visitor says. 'It's an eagle.'

'Of course it's a chicken,' comes the reply. 'It walks, talks and eats like a chicken. It even thinks like a chicken.'

'No, man,' the visitor persists. 'It's not a chicken. Let me show you.' And the visitor takes the bird and holds it above his head. 'Fly, eagle, fly,' he shouts, as the eagle stretches forth its wings.

Looking about however at the chickens feeding in the farm yard the eagle jumps down to join them. 'I told you, it was a chicken,' says the farmer. And everyone laughs. The next day the visitor comes back to the kraal and asks the farmer for a ladder. 'Give me the eagle,' he says as he stands the ladder next to the farmer's hut. 'I'll show you that it's an eagle.'

So the visitor takes the eagle and sets it on top of the farmer's hut. 'Man,' he says, 'you aren't a chicken, you're an eagle. You belong to the heavens not to the earth. Fly, eagle, fly.' The eagle stretches its wings and looks around for a moment. But then it slides down the thatched roof to the ground to eat up the scraps on which the other chickens are feeding. And everyone laughs again at the foolishness of the visitor.

A few days later nonetheless – very early one morning, before sunrise – the visitor returns. 'Let me have the eagle one last time,' he says. 'I'll show you that it's an eagle.' And so he takes the eagle in his arms and invites the farmer to follow him to the top of a high mountain nearby. Reaching the mountain top he carefully places the eagle on the nearest ledge far above the valley beneath. 'Man,' he says to the eagle, 'you belong to the heavens not to the earth. When the sun rises you must rise with it.'

At that moment the sun's first rays are appearing as the bird stretches forth its wings, feeling the warmth of the sun's rays. 'Fly, eagle, fly,' shouts the visitor. All is silent as the eagle sits perched on the ledge. And then suddenly, feeling a draught of wind which catches its wings the eagle is swept into flight – higher and higher into the skies – never again to live among the chickens.

I'm sure you'll agree with me that that is a wonderful story by the standards of any narrative tradition. And the response to a story is I guess silence; the silence of waiting and discernment on the mountain top; the silence which is a prelude to all real recognition and wisdom. For story – parable – can never merely be boiled down – as it so often is – to one particular meaning. A parable, as we know from our Christian tradition, is pregnant with meanings – in the plural – and these meanings we have to appropriate for ourselves if story is to have real validity and vitality. But at the risk of destroying the magic – the mystery – of the story I have just told, allow me now to reflect with you on some of the meanings for us as Anglicans which we may discern for ourselves in respect of the future of our Anglican Communion.

The challenge

First, let me suggest to you that this story in fact offers us, I believe, a model for the story of our Anglican Communion itself – a story which has begun to be told but which is yet to be finished. For at one level *Fly, Eagle, Fly* is a story about how we do or do not celebrate diversity. A farmer sets off looking for his lost calf. His is a desire to unify – to reunite those for whom he has a care within one fold. Now this is no bad motive for sure. And it is a motive which is of course deeply embedded within our Anglican tradition. The Lambeth Conference itself arose out of conflict in my province over the nature of doctrinal unity – a conflict around the figure of Bishop Colenso of Natal. It thus came into being precisely through a desire to re-establish common ground, to set out common objectives and principles. And that is an important continuing goal of our Communion. But the search for unity of course often throws up surprises. The farmer went looking for a calf and what he found, instead, was an eagle. But he didn't of course recognize it as such. His only frame of reference was chickens. So he treated the eagle as a chicken. And that too, I would suggest, is also part and parcel of the continuing story of our Anglican Communion which began with the first Lambeth Conference around the Colenso controversy. For while we proclaim unity in and through diversity I'm not so sure how far we have actually embraced diversity itself. For the recent Lambeth Conference – with its bitter controversies around issues of human sexuality and the interpretation of scripture – would seem to suggest that we are in fact really struggling to recognize our diversity, let alone to embrace it. We are, as my fellow South African, Professor Denise Ackerman, suggested to the Conference, failing to deal with perceived 'otherness' in as creative a way as possible. In this sense we are treating eagles as chickens and preventing them from flying as God wills them to fly.

At another level, this story is about what we might term the 'conformity of oppression'. And by this I mean to direct your attention to that central part of the story where the visitor comes to the farmer's kraal to inform him that what he supposed to be a chicken is really an eagle. For that input from the outside is, I would suggest, symbolic of another – more painful – part of the story of our Anglican Communion. In the quest for unity – for conformity of doctrine and belief and practice – laudable though all three of these may be – has too often involved those at the centre of the Communion being sent out to the kraals and villages of far-flung places to correct perceptions and frankly to tell others how things must be with and for them. In raising this issue of colonialism I know that I am entering very difficult territory, territory which often raises the hackles of many people. But difficult though this issue is that is not a reason for ignoring it. And in this sense there are some very real questions which we must ask of our Anglican Communion and its structures and systems of affiliation and governance. For while the prevalent historical, missionary model of Anglicans moving out from the first to the two-thirds world to correct misperceptions of belief and doctrine and practice may have been reversed over recent years – by a recognition that the balance of membership of our Communion has, for instance, shifted hugely to the southern hemisphere – the vestiges of neo-colonialism and paternalism nonetheless remain enshrined in our Anglican institutions, and in our instruments of dialogue and unity.

In this sense I would want us all to take a long look at the Lambeth Conference itself and to ask of it a series of interrelated questions. Is it morally defensible, for instance, in a diverse, global context that representatives of our family should return to the perceived 'motherland' for the conference? Is it appropriate, furthermore, that the conference should be called together by the Archbishop of Canterbury? Is it right in a Communion claiming to advocate democratic structures that we continue to centralize administrative resources in the old – or indeed new – colonial centres of the first world? Or that we only invite bishops to consult on the great matters of the day? Would it not in fact be more appropriate, desirable and representative for the Lambeth Conference – a reshaped Conference embracing elected representatives of laity, clergy and bishops – to meet in different contexts? And would we not in fact furthermore express a more realistic sense of unity in diversity if we instituted a rotating presidency of the Communion – not unlike the rotating presidency of the European Union? For while (as in another case, that of the Commonwealth) we could preserve the historic role of the Archbishop of Canterbury as a visible focus for the Communion, a rotating presidency would liberate us from the unhelpful centralizing stereotypes which continue, I believe, to hold back many Anglicans from full participation and recognition within our Communion. In the context of *Fly, Eagle, Fly!* wouldn't it be wonderful – and liberating then – if we all had the opportunity to experience what it feels like to be the visitor rather than merely the visited (historically, in colonial terms, the harangued and hectored) and thus to learn, as we must, how it is that together all of us are to assist one another to fly with eagles' wings. For while as my story makes plain there is a bottom line – an eagle is an eagle and not a chicken; there are basics of belief and practice and doctrine from which we may not swerve – the way in which we re-learn these basics is, I would submit, not through any vestigial or lingering sense of their being dispensed to us from the centre but by their being reformulated in the particularities of our contexts. We need then really to recognize the validity and vibrancy of these contexts and to enshrine such a recognition in our institutions. In this regard, an enhanced Anglican Consultative Council, more representative, gender-sensitive and also involving our young people – as a dynamic means of consultation – based perhaps in a two-thirds world context and funded by the richer members of the Communion would be a good place to continue the necessary process of our transformation from colonial to global Communion. It could also be a symbol of our desire more equably to distribute the resources of the Communion more equally and so to achieve the kind of opportunity for real liberation from dependency which should be our goal for Anglicans everywhere.

The Archbishop of Canterbury has played a leading role here – not least in setting up the Anglican Communion Fund. What I am advocating therefore is, I believe, simply a logical extension of the unfolding story of our Communion. And in this what I am most seeking to do is to advocate the kind of liberating opportunities which my story from Ghana pin-points so clearly. For if you want an eagle to fly – and not to remain (or be perceived to remain) as a chicken – you have not merely to hold it above your head or stick it on your roof – where you can still keep an eye on it – you have actually to let go of it, risk leaving it at the top of a mountain and give it a realistic chance to achieve that of which it is undoubtedly capable. True growth and development are made possible by the creation of genuine opportunities for flight. And this is, I believe, what our sisters and brothers across the Communion most desire and need. They love the Communion; they love the bonds of affection which tie us one to another; they have huge respect for the office – and person – of the Archbishop of Canterbury which has historically embodied Anglicanism for all of us. But they also sense – many of them in and through situations of abject poverty – that the riches of this Church will only truly be unlocked – the eagle will only learn finally to fly – through a liberation from the negative aspects of our Communion's story – through our true structural liberation into that freedom which is within our grasp if we can allow the Spirit to lift us beyond existing models and methods of mission. For ours is already a great story, a story of friendship and unity which has changed the lives of millions across the world. But it is also a story much of which still needs to be told, as we seek to fulfil our calling as Christ's disciples and to liberate all people into the fullness of God's kingdom.

SCRIPTURE: WHAT IS AT ISSUE IN ANGLICANISM TODAY?

If this section raises more questions than it answers, I shall be well satisfied. In my exploration of this topic, the more I have delved into the questions, the less sure I feel about any of the answers. That, for me, is good theology. But it should serve as a warning to those who want sure and certain truths, that I am not going to meet that need here.

There are two ambiguous words in the title: scripture and Anglicanism. We assume that we know what they mean, but I do not think it is all that clear. For example, when we talk of scripture do we mean the Old and New Testaments? The Apocrypha? The non-canonical texts? Commentaries on and interpretations of the foregoing?

Then there is the tricky question of what is meant by Anglicanism. What is its essence? Is there something definitively 'Anglican'? Can we even point to varieties of 'Anglicanisms'? Anglicanism grew out of the Reformation in England. In other words, it was formed and developed in a particular context. Though the context remained quite similar for several centuries, there has now been a radical shift from the context of Anglicanism's roots. One used to be able to point to the prayer book as the central essence, but in the last 40 years or so there have been many new translations of the texts and revisions of the liturgy in various parts of the Communion, as we attempt to culturize the prayer book and translate it into languages other than English. This process of inculturation has diluted or removed altogether the colonial English church. I am not suggesting this is to be deplored. Far from it. But it raises questions as to what is definitively Anglican. Are we simply to acknowledge that anyone who wishes to be called Anglican should be recognized as such? This is the debate surrounding the so-called 'continuing' Anglican churches, which oppose women's ordination.

As if these questions were not difficult enough, we are faced with our rapidly changing global context. Though the Church is slow, even unwilling, to recognize it, our context is now post-modern and that influences our attitudes to the reading of scripture and the question of authority – issues we will examine in more detail.

Then there are issues which were twentieth-century phenomena and which have, depending on one's perspective, revolutionized, reformed or severely harmed the Church: the feminist movement, the growing recognition of the place of inter-faith dialogue and the issues debated most fiercely by the last two Lambeth Conferences, namely the ordination of women, and the place of homosexual people.

The question of authority of scripture

Throughout the history of the Anglican Church, scripture has played a pivotal role in the Church's theological discourse and liturgical practice. The Constitution of my own Province states that it 'receives and maintains the Faith of our Lord Jesus Christ as taught in the Holy Scriptures'. This underlines the fact that the importance of the scriptures cannot be disregarded. In fact scripture is regarded as a primary source for studying and practising theology, along with reason, faith, culture, experience and tradition. However, although this is the formal position of the Church – namely that scripture is one source among several others – it is certainly not reflected in terms of practice, where greater weight tends to be given to scripture. For instance, in the case of the debate around homosexuality, scripture was used

113

as the predominant standard, against which the different positions in the debate were measured. A significant number of bishops (arguing both for and against the acceptance of homosexuality and homosexual practice) based their arguments upon the Old and New Testaments where, prima facie, homosexual practice is condemned.

This debate has focused attention on fundamental questions relating to scripture, its authority and its interpretation. It is these questions to which we now turn as we search to find the significance of scripture for us today.

1 What constitutes scripture? This is not a simple question. There is no agreement as to what constitutes scripture. For example what is the position of the Apocryphal writings? What is the position of those writings which are not generally included even in the Apocrypha such as the Story of Norea, the daughter of Eve, and the Gospel of Mary, which present us with alternative frameworks?

2 Can the social-cultural ethos out of which the writings emerged and in which they served as a liberating directive for the readers of their time, be used in our contexts today in a way that is liberating?

3 Who determines, and how, whether scripture is authoritative or not in relation to contemporary challenges facing us, such as gender and sexual orientation?

4 Which interpretations of scripture take precedence today in the church? The traditional interpretation of theologians and clerics? The current contemporary interpretations coming from marginalized groups (based on gender, race, culture, social-economic factors, sexual orientation)?

There are, in broad terms, three different positions, which are upheld within contemporary Anglicanism with regard to calling upon scripture as a source of authority.

First, there are those who see scripture as the one and only source of authority. Here the text is used as a literal proof-text. This approach is aptly demonstrated by the story of a woman who believed that giving birth almost yearly was how she should respond to God's injunction to increase and multiply (Genesis 1.28).

Second, there are those who see it as one source among others. In other words they do not see scripture as authoritative on its own. We need to place scripture alongside experience, reason, culture, faith and tradition. For example, if one were to place these sources on a continuum, ranging from scripture on the one hand to tradition on the other – one would then have the different variable placed in between. For feminist theologians who use the oral and written experiences of women as the predominant sources for doing theology, the continuum might begin with experience, then faith, and somewhere along the line scripture will appear. For feminist theologians what may be most important is interpretation of praxis over against, or in the light of, scripture.

Third, there are those who do not see scripture as the authoritative source at all. It is simply another text to be considered. For example, some Christians outside the western world, with their own cultural orientation, see scripture as no more authoritative than other religious myths, gods, goddesses and legends.

Are these three positions mutually exclusive? If one chooses one position does this mean that one has nothing to say or hear from those who adopt different stances?

If one takes the first position, namely a literal reading of the scripture as the authoritative source for doing theology (what we would loosely call fundamentalism) one would not countenance the views of those who took the second and third positions. In other words dialogue would not be possible. However, for those who see scripture as one course among others, whatever weight one gave to scripture, there would be a basis for some sort of dialogue. The relationship between these three stances and the possibility or otherwise for dialogue becomes important as we move to consider the issue of authority.

Therefore we have to recognize an essential and continuing tension between (1) the witness of scripture and (2) the Church's context, life and teaching. It is this that gives vitality both to the Church and to scripture. Many writers have stressed the existentialist position that the context and attitude of the interpreter have a deep effect on the meaning of the text. The African in a situation of poverty gives a different meaning to the text from that provided by an affluent believer in the USA. The meaning does not reside simply in the text but in the reader's view of the text. Is one more correct than the other?

The importance of the Bible is that it provides a common reference point for all Christian people. It is a guide to life (not a law-book), and its meaning and authority has to be worked out by the local Christian community. In this sense the authority of the Church and that of the Bible go hand in hand, and the Bible's authority has to be freely accepted.

The question of authority in the Anglican Communion

One of the interesting side effects of the Lambeth debates on the ordination of women in 1988 and on homosexuality in 1998, has been a fresh look at the question of authority in Anglicanism. In those provinces where there is a disagreement with the majority stance taken on the homosexuality issue, people have been at pains to stress that decisions taken at Lambeth have no binding authority on any bishop or province in the Communion. Those bishops in the majority have not argued to the contrary. However, some, including the Archbishop of Canterbury, have urged bishops to display unity and not to 'go it alone'. The issue is of course much broader and deeper than simply the debate on homosexuality. It goes to a fundamental question within Anglicanism: the nature and extent of authority. That is not a new question.

The nature of authority

Authority 'refers to the capacity someone has to commend free assent to another' (Yarnold 1981). Yarnold stresses that the word 'free' is essential, and for this reason authority is not synonymous with power. However, the two cannot be divorced. Authority suggests the legitimate use of power. Legitimization may arise from agreement between those who have power and those who do not; or it may arise in a less mutual way. What is important is the recognition that authority implies relationship and is a dynamic process rather than a static rule. That this is so is evidenced by the changing attitudes towards all forms of authority (both ecclesial and secular) in the past 40 years.

The Lambeth Conference of 1948 argued that authority is grounded in the life of the Trinity, and that all other authority is secondary. I have recently come across a model proposed by David Cunningham, in his book on Trinitarian theology. On the basis of the Trinitarian relationship he suggests a relationship of persuasion rather than power or coercion. Cunningham distinguishes persuasion (which is committed to non-violence) from coercion, or compulsion, with which he associates violence, oppression and force.

The 1948 Lambeth Conference went on to argue that secondary authority is distributed interactively between a variety of elements including scripture, reason, tradition, the creeds, ministry, the witness of the saints and the *consensus fidelium,* thus excluding any one of these secondary authorities from claiming primary status. Such understanding furthermore reinforces the understanding of the dynamic, relational nature of authority. An interesting observation on this dynamic interaction is made by Stephen Sykes, who suggests that conflict is a probability in such a persuasive, interactional model of authority (Sykes 1978, p. 87).

Cunningham's model of persuasion is, I want to suggest, peculiarly apposite for the Anglican situation. The Anglican Church, unlike the Roman Catholic Church, has no formal teaching authority. There is no one body or organ charged with maintaining 'sacred doctrine'. Indeed it is a moot point whether there is any such thing as 'core doctrine' in Anglicanism (see, for example, Hefling 1998 p. 233) On the other hand, unlike some of the other Protestant Churches, the Anglican Church does not recognize scripture as the only authority. With multiple sources of authority (as recognized above) there are three possibilities: coercion, ostracism or persuasion.

If this Trinitarian model of persuasion were to be adopted, what would some of the consequences be for the way we are Church? Cunningham suggests three significant consequences: first, multiple voices would be heard. Second, there would be an 'interweaving' of the lives of those in authority with others. Third, we would recognize the need for holding a space for particularity or difference.

Episcopal authority

The place of episcopal authority has come under the spotlight more recently with the ARCIC statement *The Gift of Authority*, and the Anglican Consultative Council has referred this document for study and discussion. The document, however, operates from the assumption that authority and power are synonymous. The authority referred to in *The Gift of Authority* is primarily the authority of the Pope. What, though, would Cunningham's model of persuasion suggest for episcopal authority? I believe our current model, and the model presupposed by the ARCIC document, is challenged by Cunningham's vision of persuasion. However, Cunningham's vision does not exclude episcopacy. What is excluded is the model of authority that suggests the Church speak with 'one voice' from a fixed foundation of 'truth'. What is also excluded is the model of authority which gives power to one who is removed (either geographically or relationally) from the local context.

I will use the model of persuasion as a basis for considering some of the issues facing the Anglican Communion.

Inculturation

One of the key issues, not only for the Anglican Church, but also for the Church in Africa generally, is the issue of Africanization.

The need for the indigenization and Africanization of the Church in Africa has long been recognized. It has been felt all the more since most of the African countries have been decolonized and since South Africa held its first democratic election in 1994. Earlier African theologians began by condemning missionaries' involvement in colonial rule, denigration of traditional rites and customs, attitudes of racial superiority and of paternalism, and an

117

unhappy desire to keep the African Church for as long as possible under European rule. Some African theologians have proceeded in the search of African expressions of Christianity in terms of the need for Christianity to free itself from the influences of the colonial and apartheid eras. Thus they grapple with the relationship between Christian faith and political power. The liberation approach became a dominant model in this regard, and was popularized especially by theologians from the south. Other African theologians like John Mbiti sought to relate the Christian faith to African culture and tradition. In theological circles inculturation or indigenization has become the defining aspect of this approach. Yet others have argued for a symbiosis of both approaches. In all approaches the use of scripture was of significant essence, albeit with different viewpoints.

Misapplication of scripture

Early attempts at moving towards the Africanization of Christianity using the inculturation model applied the methods learnt from the early missionaries and colonialists, such as the use of scripture as a primary text. All things to be included in the Christian fold had to be justified on scriptural grounds. Theologians who have used this approach include John Mbiti, Edward Fashole-Luke and Kwesi Dickson. Fashole-Luke for example stated that biblical categories had to be 'translated into the social milieu and thought forms of the African continent'. The major weakness of this approach is that it sought to dress Christianity in African culture while maintaining its foreignness in terms of symbols, thought forms and value systems. In practice this implied the adaptation of the European practices and thought patterns to the cultural life of the people of Africa.

Even more objectionable is the assumption that scripture has independence from the culture in which it is read, and therefore has authority over African traditions and values. It echoes the prevalent but unacceptable presumption that the north knows better what is best for the south. Scripture became a tool of domination in the sense that African Christians could not escape the colonial models of being Christian. All models of Christianity came from outside, rather than inside Africa. The approach was intended to maintain the status quo even though the model was used by the African theologians themselves. Oppression through colonial domination has been internalized. Models of 'being church' remained hierarchical and colonial.

In an article entitled 'Is There an African Democracy?' Herbert Vilakazi, a South African academic and member of the Independent Electoral Commission, reminds us that a similar uncritical incorporation of western-style government has resulted in post-colonial African governments slavishly following western models rather than drawing on truly African understandings of community and government.

Misapplication of local cultures as the primary source

Another shift took place when African culture and tradition were treated as the primary source alongside the Bible, largely as a result of liberation theology in the 1960s. Theologians such as Parratt, Mosala and Manas Buthelezi exemplified this shift. It opened the canon of scripture to include the stories and myths of African people as valid and authoritative texts for doing theology in Africa.

The value of this model is that it began to undermine some of the colonial models of being church, for example by assuming that one does not have to go via England in order to come to Africa. The weakness of the model is that it continued to maintain patriarchy in the sense that it was unable to critique patriarchal models and so it was self-defeating. Leadership in the church in Africa has remained almost exclusively in the hands of men. This is well illustrated by the example of the debate at Lambeth 1988 and 1998 on the issue of polygamy. Here was an attempt to re-incorporate an aspect of many African cultures, without any regard at all to the voice of African women.

Feminist critique of the use of scripture

Significant contributions by women in the Church in Africa began to be heard in the 1990s. Previously women were not only excluded from theological discourse, but they were even excluded from theological education. Having entered the debate, the feminist critique reminds us trenchantly of how patriarchal are our models of the interpretation of scripture. The feminist call for a different way of 'being church' looks towards inclusivity.

During the colonial period the principal actors were the foreign missionaries. They were followed by Africans who still used the European way of doing things. This then gave way to a model which moved to an African way of doing 'church'. In turn this model was criticized by the feminist theologians who pointed out that women were excluded from the circle. If we are to be truly inclusive, we need all these voices, together, rather than to replace one set of actors by another.

Symbolism

Whereas the colonial models, which intended to entrench control, were monocultural and exclusive, inculturation has come to mean not so much

119

the revocation of non-African ways of being, but rather the inclusion of the tradition of the Church while at the same time rooting its practice in the symbols and traditions of Africa. For example the Christian symbol of the cross, while not especially African, is central to Christianity and stands at the centre of African Christian worship. Where contextualization has taken place is in the replacing of the Caucasian-featured Jesus on the cross with an African figure.

If we look back to Cunningham's model of persuasion we might note the following:

1 All the voices of Africa – including missionaries, local people, women and men – are needed in order to develop a truly African Christianity.
2 Both the tradition and contemporary symbols and interpretations are needed.
3 There is no single definitive version of contextualized Christianity. There will be as many variations as there are many influences and voices.

Sexuality and gender

The next issue to which we turn, like the issue of inculturation, is not an issue peculiar to the Anglican Church. It has, however, been given added prominence in the Anglican Communion since the 1998 Lambeth Conference. One of the major issues at the conference was the issue of homosexuality. The discussion centred on the place of homosexual persons in the Church and the way the Church should respond to homosexual persons in their chosen lifestyle – for example those who seek the Church's blessing on their union, or those who seek ordination.

I do not want to rehearse the arguments again. However, those debates offer three significant insights in the context of this chapter:

1 We might note the reliance on scripture to support a position condemning homosexuality per se, or homosexual activity specifically. Those who are convinced that homosexuality is sinful, or at best a lamentable condition which requires of homosexual persons a commitment to lifelong celibacy, point to scripture as self-evidently clear on the issue. Biblical texts were seldom examined in their context. The understanding of homosexuality in biblical times was not explored, or even questioned as being different from our own understandings. In the light of the three positions identified when we looked at the authority of scripture, this acceptance of the biblical positions falls in the first or second of the two categories: namely, that scripture needs no interpretation; or second

that it needs interpretation and those condemning homosexuality have the authority to interpret the scripture in the way they have done. In other words, it was assumed that the Bible spoke clearly on the issue and that homosexuality is sinful at worst, or at best is a condition which calls for lifelong celibacy from those who are homosexual. Given that the scriptures were written at least 19 centuries ago, before the advent and development of our current medical, psychological and sociological studies, this attitude towards scripture might validly be accused of being simply a way to support a particular prejudice.

2 The second insight offered by the Lambeth debates derives from the obvious failure to look towards, let alone rely upon, other sources for doing theology – sources such as reason, tradition, culture, and most significantly experience. Most of us are aware of the embarrassing refusal of the Lambeth group tasked with looking at the issue to listen to the stories of homosexual persons. However, it was not simply that the experience of homosexual persons was ignored. Medical and psychological evidence was not considered either.

3 Finally there was no hesitation is assuming that Lambeth had the right (indeed some would say the obligation) to make a pronouncement on the issue. In other words, it was simply assumed that the bishops of the Anglican Communion had the right to make a decision as to how homosexual persons are to be received (or not, as the case may be) within the Communion. Unlike Cunningham's persuasion model, there was no consultation with the wider Church and no engaging in debate with local congregations on their experiences.

In this emotive issue, as in similar issues, there appears to be a conscious or unconscious weighing in favour of the Bible as the primary source, an acceptance that 'ultimate truth' is to be discovered in scripture. This despite the Anglican assurance that theology is derived from a number of sources.

As we grapple with these issues perhaps we need to take note of what Canon John Suggit said in his book *The Word of God and the People of God*, where he suggested that we need to discover the leading themes of the scriptures which can help control our interpretation. Canon Suggit suggested that these are the loving faithfulness of God, and God's righteousness, resulting in effect in the supremacy of the two commandments of love of God and love of others. Others have suggested such themes as liberation and mercy as providing the key to interpretation. In this way we may be helped to let the local context become so important as to outweigh the universal appeal of scripture.

Doubtless, we have to be aware of the danger of allowing such diverse interpretations of scripture as would render the faith of one Anglican province so different from another as to be unrecognizable. That was the problem in the early Church which led to a definition of heresy, and which put the Church's faith into a straitjacket.

Conclusion

How has the Lambeth decision impacted on the Anglican provinces around the world? At a world-wide level it has highlighted divisions in the Communion. The pleas by a number of bishops for unity in the Communion evidence the recognition of this division. In my own context in the Church of the Province of Southern Africa, the decision has similarly divided people. Some are pleased that the Church has taken a 'strong stand' against homosexuality. Others feel that an injustice has been perpetrated. More than any other issue of our time, this one has served to illustrate the wide difference between us in theology, in theological method, in the use of scripture, in our response to authority and how that authority is defined.

The issue of homosexuality is not alone though in highlighting our differences. The debates at Lambeth in regard to inter-faith dialogue, for example, have similarly exposed our very different approaches.

Underlying these differences is the unspoken but ever-present challenge to examine what exactly we mean by authority in our post-modern context. I am not suggesting a movement into anarchic anti-authoritarianism, but a critical questioning of what Cunningham describes as a fixed foundation of truth giving rise to one voice. We are coming to recognize more and more that institutional authority is never independent of those who invest a person or body with that authority. To put it bluntly, bishops are authoritative in the church as long as the members of the church assent to allowing that authority to persist.

Does this suggest that Cunningham's model of persuasion is not just a nice alternative, but indeed the only viable model if we are to hold on to one another in our differences? Is the challenge to us, with all our differences and questions, to seek out in conversation with one another that which is good, healthy and life-giving, with all the risk that that implies in having to let go of old securities? If this is our challenge it is indeed a radical one; but so too of course is the gospel.

FOUR

New Perspectives

The horrific tragedy of 11 September 2001 has challenged us all to examine the future shape of our world. For the first time a single event has dramatically illustrated how vulnerable and mutually dependent we are in this, our global village.

The destruction of the twin Trade towers, the hub of global economic activity, and the attack on the Pentagon, the nerve centre of military might of the world's superpower, have been analysed and debated *ad nauseam*. The indisputable fact which emerges is that a supreme challenge has been posed: work together for the common good or perish!

At the time I wrote:

As citizens of our global world we were horrified, shocked and mesmerized by the tragic events that took place in New York and Washington. Such atrocious acts can only be attributed to a deadly fanaticism which leads people to commit such horrendous crimes against humanity.

Equally, we are extremely confounded by the massive military response from the world's superpower and the extensive destruction to the lives of innocent and long oppressed Afghanistanis who have not been given an opportunity to be heard and against whom exists no conclusive evidence of complicity. There is a pervasive sense of fear, loss and confusion as to the future direction of the affairs of the world.

One thing we do know, and should never lose sight of, is that in actions like these it is people who are affected. When a child is killed in Palestine, a secretary is crushed beneath the rubble of a building in New York, a family is bombed in Afghanistan – the whole of creation bleeds. We must recognize that no war is holy. All war is evil. It kills and maims people. And the fact is that after every war the protagonists end up talking. Why can't the talk simply replace destruction?

Now that the dust is beginning to settle and emotions have relatively subsided, it is time for us to recommit ourselves unreservedly to reconciliation and sustainable world peace. Otherwise we will all be destroyed by the pervasive evils of fear and hate.

We must look beyond the tragic events of 11 September. We need visionary, imaginative and creative leadership that will work relentlessly towards eliminating conditions that feed the dangerous fanaticism that exists worldwide today. We need leadership that will make the world a safe and secure environment for all citizens. In this regard I would like to propose the following:

1 One of the fundamental tenets of a democracy is maintenance of the rule of law. We must at all times avoid the temptation of revenge. History has shown that violence begets violence. In our world today we need a well resourced, effective and efficient international criminal justice system that is swiftly able to bring to account perpetrators of heinous crimes against humanity.

2 We need to recognize that 'to God belongs the earth and all who live therein' (Psalm 24.1). As stewards of his creation this places on us an obligation to care for one another and to ensure that there is equitable sharing of resources so that everyone has the basics for life with dignity, such as food, shelter, clothing, water, health care and education.

3 In the governance of our global village we need to ensure that there is equity, transparency and responsibility.

There are in existence already certain international instruments or bodies which were created to maintain order and stability in the world. The devastation of two world wars prompted men and women to look for positive and practical ways to ensure lasting world peace. The United Nations is one visible result of this search. But we know now, more than ever before, that the search is by no means over. In our quest for peace and resolution of conflict, bodies such as the UN need to be re-appraised and strengthened. After all humans are by nature social animals; it is of our essence that we should live in peaceful relation with one another and this fact needs to be underlined constantly.

Never again can we accept the surreal situation in which a superpower simultaneously drops bombs and food parcels on an already debilitated nation. More importantly, we must not allow the economic, political and social injustices that have throughout history bred fanaticism. We must think and act as citizens of the world – the old divides of north and south or east and west can no longer apply.

Some may argue that this is wishful thinking and that humankind is not adept at learning from its mistakes. This is not so. Much goodwill exists. In recent decades we have experienced huge advances in terms of negotiated politics, industrial relations, strategic partnerships and even shared currencies, like the euro. In countries such as my own we have come to value and build on the richness that comes from diversity. In the religious arena inter-faith cooperation, dialogue and advocacy is gaining momentum. In an environment that thrives on bad news, the good is too often overlooked.

After years of being labelled naive and impractical, those of us who have consistently campaigned for the cancellation of international debt owed by the developing countries are greatly heartened by the decision among some G8 countries to cancel all of what is owed. These countries, along with several leading economists, finally acknowledge that 'business as usual' is not in their own interest – that greed and self-interest have created an imbalance that endangers the entire world economy. Those countries that have seen the light can and must use their influence on others. This is not so difficult as national leaders increasingly co-operate on global issues.

Hopefully economic leadership is also coming to realize that people are not poor because they choose to be, or are too lazy or too stupid or too culturally skewed to do something about it. They are poor because they operate in an environment that has been exploited to the point of paralysis. They are poor because they live in a world of surplus resources inequitably distributed.

In the non-governmental and non-commercial horizon, the Jubilee 2000 movement has made great strides in marshalling civil organizations to cooperate – especially in the role of advocacy – in a campaign to alleviate poverty.

The likes of the International Monetary Fund, the World Bank and the World Economic Forum are no longer hurtling along unchallenged.

It seems that note is finally being taken of Nobel economics laureate Professor Amartya Sen who emphasized that the validity of any economic policy should be judged on whether it takes into account its impact of people on the on the downside of an economy.

The business community – hard hit by organized crime, fraud and shady practices – is slowly, but surely, beginning to address ethical issues. There is a growing awareness that, while profit is the motivating factor in business, there is a critical need to place human values at the centre of economic systems. Every management book tells and most corporate mission statements state that the human resource is the most valuable asset of all.

Religious leaders worldwide are accepting the mantle of prophetic ministry and alerting the world at large to unjust systems. Typically, the Anglican Communion, with a constituency of more than 70 million members, is increasingly using its collective muscle to address issues such as HIV and AIDS and the unpayable debt of developing countries. Moreover, I often operate in an inter-faith arena and am greatly heartened by the mutual respect, tolerance and spiritual generosity that prevails among Jewish, Muslim, Christian, Baha'i, Buddhist and Hindu leaders.

On an individual basis, it was another Nobel prize winner, Jonas Salk, who said: 'We are the first generation in human history in which large numbers of ordinary people are taking personal responsibility for the future of the entire species.'

It is all about mutual respect and a collective inclusive responsibility and although I am optimistic, we do still have a long way to go. I remain convinced that poverty is the pivotal issue. As Mahatma Gandhi once said, 'Poverty is the worst form of violence'. Born out of avarice, indifference and a false sense of superiority, poverty flies in the face of God, in whose image all humankind is made. It is at the heart of Africa's AIDS pandemic and other health woes. Poverty, as I have said elsewhere, exists because we fail to allow people to break out of its cycle. It was the World Health Organization that pointed out several years ago that in order to acquire wealth a nation first needs healthy people – not the other way round. I would posit that the same applies to education and other social environment factors that should automatically take precedence in a national budget over arms deals and the servicing of unpayable debt.

But the single most unifying challenge remains and that is for world citizens in all walks of life – politics, business, welfare, the arts, religion, sport and entertainment – to remember how vulnerable and interdependent we all felt after the US tragedy and to act accordingly. We dare not forget that we are the sum of each other; we must remember the concept of *ubuntu* (see p. 80).

Let us respond to the call of that wise African leader Julius Nyerere, who never failed to remind us of the familyhood of humankind, and let us choose to move forward together.

POSTSCRIPT: WORLD SUMMIT ON SUSTAINABLE DEVELOPMENT

South Africa hosted the 2002 World Summit on Sustainable Development. This was the largest ever UN conference: the world came to Johannesburg to face the crisis confronting humanity and the natural environment, and to try to chart a course for the future. Like so many international conferences, some have hailed this one a success, while others have dubbed it 'a summit of shameful deals'.

I believe that the Summit was neither all positive nor all negative. On the positive side:

- there was an integrated approach to development in which the relationship between environmental issues and poverty eradication was highlighted, as was the responsibility of all states;
- the removal of trade barriers was high on the agenda;
- issues previously discussed separately in various international forums were brought together;
- people who have never before had the opportunity to network were able to meet and communicate face to face.

From a negative point of view:

- very little was discussed on HIV and AIDS, which are major challenges in southern Africa;
- the absence of President Bush and concerns about war against Iraq tended to undermine other important summit issues;
- Colin Powell's arrival only on the final day of the summit could be seen as an indication of America's aloofness and her desire to go it alone regardless of the wishes of others in the world.

It is important for the Church to move environmental issues to the forefront of our agenda. I would like to pay tribute here to Bishop Geoff Davies, our liaison bishop on environmental issues. His has been a lone but persistent voice in this arena. It is he who co-ordinated the recent Anglican Conference on the Environment at Hartebeespoort Dam, north of Johannesburg. Many representatives from Provinces of the Anglican Communion attended, and a joint declaration to the UN World Summit was drawn up. It will be of great value in guiding us in our future work.

It is vital that we address the issue of the moral and ethical dimension of environmental sustainability. We need to answer the question of how this dimension is to be addressed, formulated and proclaimed in the church – denominationally, ecumenically and with those of other faiths. We need to make a solid commitment to the conservation and preservation of the earth over which God gave us dominion. True dominion is like the dominion of God, which is informed by love and carries an inherent duty to protect.

All of us must commit ourselves to a hope that refuses to accept an unjust and tarnished world order. God reigns. He wills only what is good for the world. We have a major responsibility to be committed to the survival of the global village. We need to work afresh for spiritual and moral liberation, which brings wholeness of life. The need has never been as great for people to be shown that this young millennium offers hope. It will depend both on the world's leaders and ourselves as leaders in our own small communities. We are called to act decisively and with conviction in protecting resources, working for true sustainable development and by giving the lead for a new moral order.

Select references and further reading

ARCIC statement (1999), *The Gift of Authority: Authority in the Church III: an agreed statement*, London: Catholic Truth Society.

Chossudovsky, Michel (1986), *The Globalization of Poverty: Impacts of IMF and World Bank reforms*, London: Zed Books.

Church of England, Archbishop of Canterbury's Commission on Urban Priority Areas (1985), *Faith in the City: A call for action by church and nation*, London: Church House Publishing.

Cunningham, David (1998), *These Three Are One*, Oxford: Blackwell.

Department for International Development (1997), *Eliminating World Poverty: A challenge for the 21st century*, White Paper, Stationery Office.

Fawcett, J. E. S. (1979), quoted in F. E. Dowrick (ed.) *Human Rights*, Aldershot: Ashgate Publishing.

Fletcher, Michael A., and Mufson, Steven (2000), in *Washington Post*, 17 February.

Forrester, D. B., and Skene, D., eds (1988), *Just Sharing: A Christian approach to the distribution of wealth, income and benefits*, London: Epworth.

Friedman, Thomas (2000), *The Lexus and the Olive Tree*, London: HarperCollins.

Greenslade, S. L. (1953), *Schism in the Early Church*, London: SCM Press.

Gregorowski, Christopher (2000), *Fly, Eagle, Fly!*, Cape Town: Tafelberg. This story is attributed originally to James Aggrey, a Ghanaian born in 1875.

Greider, William (1998), *One World, Ready or Not: The manic logic of global capitalism*, London: Touchstone.

Hefling, Charles (1998), 'On Core Doctrine', *Anglican Theological Review*, vol. lxxx, no. 2.

Inter Action Council, *A Universal Declaration of Human Responsibilities*.

Kaplan, Robert D. (1997), *The Ends of the Earth*, London: Papermac.

McGreal, Chris (1999), 'Nigeria: Throwing Good Money After Bad', *Mail and Guardian*, 18–24 June.

Macquarrie, John (1980), 'Rethinking natural law', in C. Curran and R. McCormick (eds), *Readings in Moral Theology, No. 2: The distinctiveness of Christian Ethics*, New York: Paulist Press.

Maritain, Jacques (1971), *The Rights of Man and Natural Law*, New York: Gordian Press.

129

Mbiti, John (1970), *New Testament Eschatology in an African Background*, London: OUP.

Nurnberger, Klaus (1999), *Prosperity, Poverty and Pollution*, London: Zed Books.

Paine, Thomas (1985), *The Age of Reason*, Amherst, NY: Prometheus Books.

Qates, Whitney J. and O'Neill, Eugene (1938), *The Complete Greek Drama*, vol. 1, New York: Random House.

Sachs, Jeffrey (1999), *The Economist*, 14 August.

Suggit, John (1994), *The Word of God and the People of God: The relation between the Bible and the Church*, Cape Town: Celebration of Faith.

Sunter, Clem (2002), *Never Mind the Millennium. What about the next 24 hours?* Cape Town: Human & Rousseau Tafelberg.

Suzman, Helen (1994), *In No Uncertain Terms*, London: Mandarin.

Sykes, Stephen (1978), *The Integrity of Anglicanism*, London: Mowbray.

Vilakazi, H., 'Is there an African democracy?' *Daily News*, 17 May 2000.

Yarnold, E. (1981), 'Teaching with authority', *The Way*, 21,3.

Young, John E., Sachs, Aaron, and Ayres, Ed (1994), *The Next Efficiency Revolution: Creating a sustainable materials economy*, Washington, DC: Worldwatch Paper 121, Worldwatch Institute.